# A World of Difference

## Following Christ beyond Your Cultural Walls

## Thom Hopler

InterVarsity Press
Downers Grove
Illinois 60515

InterVarsity Press is the book-publishing division of Inter-Varsity Christian Fellowship,
a student movement active on campus at hundreds of universities, colleges
and schools of nursing. For information about local and regional activities, write
IVCF, 233 Langdon St., Madison, WI 53703.

Distributed in Canada through InterVarsity Press, 1875 Leslie St., Unit 10,
Don Mills, Ontario M3B 2M5, Canada.

Excerpts from "The Irregular Economy" are reprinted from TIME, The Weekly Newsmagazine;
Copyright Time Inc. 1973.

Bible quotations, unless otherwise stated, are from the Revised Standard Version of the
Bible, copyrighted 1946, 1952 © 1971, 1973.

ISBN 0-87784-747-9

Printed in the United States of America

---

**Library of Congress Cataloging in Publication Data**

Hopler, Thom, 1936-1978.
    A world of difference, following Christ beyond
your cultural wall.

    Bibliography: p.
    1. Christianity and culture.    2. Communication
(Theology)    3. Evangelistic work.    I. Title.
BR115.C8H66    1981            261            81-5781
ISBN 0-87784-747-9                        AACR2

---

| 17 | 16 | 15 | 14 | 13 | 12 | 11 | 10 | 9 | 8 | 7 | 6 | 5 | 4 | 3 | 2 | 1 |
|----|----|----|----|----|----|----|----|---|---|---|---|---|---|---|---|---|
| 95 | 94 | 93 | 92 | 91 | 90 | 89 | 88 | 87 | 86 | 85 | 84 | 83 | 32 | 81 | | |

## Foreword

Enclosing his son Jason with his arm, I see Thom leaning forward as he pointed to the Christmas Creche, carefully explaining the figures. Judi, Martha and Marcie knew their dad's full attention too, in skiing, swimming, camping or riding their first two-wheeler bike. Thom's touch on others had the feel of involvement. It was his way to include *you*. Humbly sitting with you, he shared himself.

A unique person, Thom Hopler called himself a bridge —a bridge between people, a bridge between truth and love, in action. He shared his spiritual gifts of wisdom and knowledge, grasping otherwise mysterious problems and predicting possible solutions in the mode of a prophet. Once someone told me, "He answered all my questions." Others felt the same.

As you read this book you may find a potpourri of ideas. That may be so because Thom himself was a mixture. He was like a mosaic with many pieces of truth. Yet his multifaceted vision formed a total image in an otherwise one-dimensional culture. It thrills me that the pages of writing here represent him in this way.

Marriage to such a rare bird might have been abrasive if Thom were not such a *human* person at home and outside the home. He slurped his coffee and laughed at himself in the midst of his profundity. Gentle and godly, he listened to us; he affirmed us. At an Urbana 79 meeting Pete Hammond said it completely when he spoke of Thom as one "who served me, as he served many of you."

Though he spoke softly, it was often with hard truth. Though he wore a gray suit, his ideas were radically sharp. May this book be the same.

Marcia Hopler

# Publisher's Preface

We at InterVarsity Press first met Thom Hopler when he attended our Writers' Workshop in August 1977. There we worked with him to develop his material on the book of Acts (much of which is found in chapters six and seven of this book).

At the time we hoped his Acts material might be published as a pamphlet. But more work was needed. So we transcribed tapes of other talks Thom had given on Acts and did preliminary editing. His response to our work was positive. We asked him to send more tapes on other subjects, and he did. We also made plans to tape, transcribe and edit more material during his speaking engagements in the summer of 1978. He never gave those talks. Thom Hopler died of a heart attack on June 12, 1978.

After consulting with his wife, Marcia, and some of Thom's friends, we decided to search for other tapes by Thom, collect his writings and notes, transcribe the tapes and evaluate all the material for possible publication. This was done. The result is the book you now hold.

As a publisher, our goal has been to make the book far more than a collection of talks and papers. We have sought to make it a single, complete and well-reasoned presentation.

The material in this book is entirely based on Thom's work and thought. The organization of the chapters and of the material within some of the chapters is, however, the result of our work in consultation with Marcia Hopler and others. The transcribed talks have also been edited to transform the material from spoken to written form. We have conscientiously sought to maintain Thom's "voice" and perspective throughout and have had the manuscript checked carefully by those who knew Thom's ministry best. Because Thom cannot himself read this book, however, it is possible that his thinking has, on occasion, been misrepresented. The responsibility for such errors is ours.

This book does not represent the totality of Thom's work. It is possible that other publications will appear under his name. But we believe it does represent the core of his thought.

We are especially grateful for the cooperation of Marcia Hopler at every stage of the production of this book. We also acknowledge the help and counsel of Neil Rendall, the regional director of Inter-Varsity Christian Fellowship in New York—New Jersey and Thom's supervisor while he was on staff with IVCF. Many others sent us tapes, notes and papers from Thom, read the final manuscript for us, and offered their suggestions along the way. We are thankful for these as well.

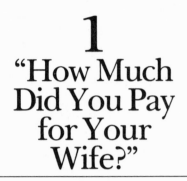

# 1
## "How Much Did You Pay for Your Wife?"

"HOW MUCH DID YOU PAY for your wife?" the old man asked during the first month Marcia and I spent in Kenya. When I explained that we don't sell women in America, he laughed and said, squeezing Marcia's thin arm, "I wouldn't give a goat for her either."

People are different. Not only do individuals differ from one another, but groups of people differ as well. On another occasion in my first months in Africa, I waved hello to a friend across the street. Immediately he ran over to me asking, "What's the matter? What do you want?" I spent the next ten minutes trying to talk my way out of that innocent cultural misstep. My hand signal did not mean "Hello," but "Come here quickly. I need you."

Crossing cultures is difficult enough by itself. But when a person is a Christian who wants to communicate the life-giving message about Jesus, the difficulty is greatly multiplied. What is culture? How does it affect my Christian life, my evangelism? What are the implications of culture for the church at large? In this chapter I want to introduce some preliminary responses to these questions and to set the stage for fuller answers in the rest of the book.

## A Garbage Truck Is Culture

Because of differing geographies, differing histories, differing climates and differing languages, different groups have developed different cultures. The word *culture* is often used in the narrow sense of "high culture"—opera, sculpture and the like. But I am using the word in a broader sense that includes the total pattern of human life in society. That means garbage trucks, radios and paper bags are all a part of culture, at least Western culture. Whether we realize it or not, much of what we do is the result of our own culture.

This has profound implications for the church as it carries the gospel from one culture to another. How much of what we teach is culture and how much is gospel? Often we simply do not know because we have never thought about what our own culture is like.

Though the concept of culture is rich and complex, I want to focus on four specific aspects. First, culture is *a mental roadmap*. It helps us get from morning to night without running into dead ends or roadblocks. Those who have been in another culture know how terribly hard it is to get up in the morning and think, "What's the first thing I say when I meet someone? And if she responds, what do I say next? And if she offers to do a favor for me, what does it mean?" You realize that every movement, everything you wear, everything you say has a certain meaning that you have to make a conscious effort to figure out. The strain this can cause is called culture shock.

Our culture teaches us how to act in standard ways in normal situations. We do not have to think about what we are to do with forks and spoons and knives when we sit down to eat. Our culture has trained us. It has given us a series of short cuts so we can function at a basic level every day. If two people from two different cultures were alone on a desert island, within weeks they would develop a third culture that would give them short cuts for dealing with one another.

*The sum total of our lived experience* is another way of looking at culture. You may not know how to play the violin, but it is part of your culture if you recognize and appreciate it when you hear it. The five-toned flute of India, on the other hand, may sound strange to your ears. While it and the music an Indian plays on it may be just as sophisticated as violin music, you think it is peculiar because it is not part of your experience, not part of your culture.

Culture also provides us with *a system of values that directs our activities.* These are not absolute within each culture. Some people always insist on "breaking the rules." And cultures will often have slightly different values for different age groups, economic classes, localities or working groups. We allow children to act in a way adults are not to act.

Values (priorities in life) are important for Christians, of course, because God, too, has values that he wants us to learn. He does not wish simply to destroy the values of our culture or any culture and replace it with a "Christian" culture. Rather he wants to add to and redirect our values.

In this sense, culture is a gift from God that can keep us from destroying ourselves. It helps us maintain a low level of sociability until God is able to lift us to a higher level by his Word. From the very beginning God has built such protection into culture, as we will see in more detail in the next chapter.

This idea is illustrated by an incident from the early 1960s. There was a movement in Africa to remove anything associated with colonialism, including Christianity. The parliament of Kenya debated this issue quite seriously. At one point a non-Christian in the parliament said, in essence, "We are a tribalistic people. We each have our own gods, our own ideals, our own understandings of right and wrong. But these are not adequate to meet the needs of our nation. With Christianity has come a system of values that supersedes tribalism. We hold our young people accountable on the basis of the Bible. If we take away the Bible, whose tribal system will we adopt in its place?"

The parliament agreed. The people had stopped killing each other because the Bible said, "Thou shalt not kill." As they discussed it further, they decided to make it mandatory to teach the Bible in all the schools in Kenya. Other religions have come into competition with Christianity, but they still require that some more universal system of values be taught. They recognize that without values, people become dangerous. God does not desire to destroy our values but to lift them to a higher plane.

The opposite is happening in the West. As we secularize and move away from biblical values, we are finding it more and more difficult to maintain order, to maintain even a low level of sociability. Thus we should not encourage other cultures simply to dump their values, which allow for a degree of peace. Rather we should show a better way.

## With Culture, Some Things Are Impossible
Lastly, culture defines for us *the limits of possibility*. For many years the four-minute mile was a barrier that people said could not be broken. It was impossible. Yet within two years after Roger Bannister ran a mile in 3 minutes 59.4 seconds, a half-dozen others did the same. It was no longer impossible.

In Africa, one of my students belonged to the Watusi tribe which averages between seven and eight feet in height.

During track practice one day the coach was struggling to help the high jumpers over the 6' 3" mark. The Watusi student, who was only seven feet tall, was standing to the side, arms folded, watching these efforts. He had never seen anything like it. But finally he asked the coach if he could try. So he walked up to the bar and started this Watusi dance which required keeping his whole body stiff except for his feet and ankles. Soon he was bouncing two feet off the ground. Suddenly he drew his knees up, cleared the bar and came down on the other side—on his feet! From a standing position he cleared 6' 3".

What we could never get him to do, however, was to go over the bar horizontally. In his tribe they fight and throw spears from a standing position only. To him balance was very important, and you must stay erect to stay balanced. You never lie down horizontally. Consequently, it was outside his culture to do the high jump the way we see it in the Olympics. For him, it was impossible.

Culture can put similar limitations on our faith. The disciples thought feeding a huge crowd was impossible—even with two hundred days' wages. But it wasn't for Jesus.

They were limited in their understanding of what Jesus could do. In their culture—and in ours, too—no human being could perform such an act. But Jesus upset their expectations. He showed them he was more than they had thought. He had the capacity to break through such cultural limitations. This is the power and the commission that he has also given his church. If we, however, accept the limits of our culture as normative, we may also limit the gospel.

The church's temptation has always been to fall into such error. We have often emphasized the worth of every individual and the image of God in each person. Less frequently we have recognized the image of God in every group of people, every culture.

*15*

## Who Is Really Backward?

"Western culture is more civilized than African culture." So goes the standard Western judgment. But is this right? While Christianity may have had a greater impact on the one than the other, and while God's values may be more evident in one than the other, we cannot conclude that Western customs are appropriate or good to bring into other cultures. Yet read any newspaper. Are we really more advanced?

Think a moment about the old man's question about how much I paid for my wife. We find the bride price a strange, if not backward, custom. How primitive to buy wives, we say. But is it? When a man and woman are married in Africa, the giving of gifts from one family to the other binds them together. Several hundred people from one family in effect marry several hundred from another. Over the course of a year prior to the marriage, these families become acquainted and exchange gifts, which establishes communication between them. When the immediate family members finally give gifts, the marriage itself can take place. The only way divorce is possible is to return all the gifts. Therefore, because a thousand people will never agree to such a thing (they want to keep what they have), divorce is virtually unknown.

After an African explained all this to me he asked, "How do you do it in America?" I explain that often the mother of the bride meets the mother of the groom for the first time the night before the wedding. In shock he said, "Why, that's barbaric." He was right. Since then I have been to several wedding rehearsals that were quite painful. Within twenty-four hours two families were expected to put together one of the most important events in their lives, and there was no cultural procedure to make it work smoothly. Some of the bitter feelings that develop that night can take years to work out.

The notion that we are more advanced and more knowledgeable than ever before has contributed to our tendency to cut ourselves off from the past, from any cultural guidelines that might help us move into the future. Instead of having norms that help us move through minor problems, we are anchorless. Marriage, for example, becomes a series of crises.

Another factor, especially in America, clouds our ability to see God's general revelation in other cultures. This is a commitment to the idea of a melting pot, a society in which all peoples can share common values and customs. Chapter ten will expand on this. For now, suffice it to say that this has tended to blind us to the validity and vitality of cultural distinctions.

The church has not been immune to such blurred vision and ethnocentrism. But as we overcome these, new life will come to the church. As Arthur Glasser notes, "the new linkage between theologians, missionaries and national church leaders all over the world . . . will not be Western-dominated. Significant stirrings are discernible among younger intellectuals in the churches of Asia, Africa and Latin America. . . . This shall bring about the long overdue transformation of a western religion into a universal faith. . . . The deposit of truth Christ gave the disciples long ago is not confined to any one segment of the structured church."[1]

One of the reasons missions can bring life to the church as a whole is that carrying the gospel crossculturally forces us to peel off culture so that only the core gospel remains. When this purer gospel is brought back to the home churches, it brings renewal. In chapter seven we will see how Paul reported back to Jerusalem what God was doing among the Gentiles (Acts 15). The Jews suddenly got a larger view of who God is. Thus crosscultural ministry brings us as Christians to the cutting edge of cultural change because we will be pointing out where our culture has gone astray and where we have strayed.

Our cultural blindness has caused us to define missions as crossing geographical barriers with the gospel. This is the great unfinished work of the church, we say. In fact, the church has never had difficulty crossing geographic barriers. From the very day the church was born, at Pentecost, those who heard the gospel believed and were baptized, returned to their distant homes around the Mediterranean basin, in Africa and in Asia (Acts 2:5-11). The only problem was that they did not cross cultural barriers with the gospel. Many of them only spoke to Jews (Acts 11:19). Indeed, Acts 8—15 records the great wrenching that had to take place before the church broke through to the Gentiles. (This is discussed more fully in chapters six and seven.) Ever since then, the church's difficulty has been to cross cultural barriers. Even today there is hardly a geographic boundary the gospel has not crossed, but there are hundreds of cultural groups which have not heard the gospel. We need new eyes to see new fields that are ready for harvest.

## Old Methods in a New Setting

Most of the experience the church has in crossing cultural barriers is in traditional foreign missions. I believe, therefore, that what missions has learned can be used profitably to reach the unreached cultures of today. We agonize over our degenerating cities, not realizing that the tools already exist to reach them for Christ. Yet many of the attitudes that prevent us from penetrating the city were identified by foreign mission experience decades ago. This book is an attempt to apply missionary insights to crosscultural evangelism.

Take one example: If missionaries have learned to live with polygamy in the church, seeking to modify it slowly rather than immediately, why have we not learned to accept the transient urban Black male in the same way?[2] We will consider this question more in the next chapter. A more important lesson is that though isolated individuals can be won for Christ, churches must be built from people involved in the community itself. Few urban ministries are aimed specifically at the average citizen.

I was in Africa for ten exciting years—1960-70—when Africa went through tremendous turmoil. It was the end of the colonial era and the beginning of independence. I became involved in the vital African church which taught me much about faith and about my own cultural limitations.

I kept hearing two disturbing questions: What is the situation of Blacks and the Black church in America? And why are there no Black missionaries from America to Africa? I had no answers, but I knew I needed some. My search took me to Newark, where the Africa Inland Mission began its first urban ministry in America. This was a radical move for a "foreign" mission society. It meant redefining its call to include all crosscultural missions, whether foreign or domestic. But it is a direction that I believe more should move in.

My search also led me to find help from a variety of places. I suspect many readers will be frustrated in their attempt to label me as having one theological stance or another, or one missions strategy or another. I have purposely avoided such labels because I seek to bridge many different groups. My concern is for the vitality of the church, and I accept insights from any source that helps God's truth to reach more and more people.

Another perspective I bring to these issues comes from sociological and anthropological urban studies. Traditionally, sociologists study social structures within a single culture while anthropologists study whole cultures and compare them to each other. Early anthropologists tended to look for the simplest and purest cultures so they could be compared most easily. Primitive and small cultures were the most likely choices for accomplishing this. Anthropologists therefore tended to avoid the city because it was so complex.

On the other hand, sociologists do not spend time dealing with cultures with only two or three institutions. They have gravitated toward complex societies—such as America. But this has created a bias because they have assumed that America is one—a complex unity, but a unity nonetheless. As this has proven untenable, sociologists have begun looking to anthropologists for help. Urban sociology and urban anthropology are similar disciplines which have developed to account for both the diversity and the interrelations found in the city. While I find help in both approaches, my bias is toward anthropology because I find the city opens up to me if I come to it with a people orientation. If I come with a system orientation, I see only confusion.

**A Look Ahead**

My goal in this book is to highlight and focus on God's concern for reaching the many different cultures of the world. I begin, in part one, by considering what the Bible has to say about crossing cultures with God's Word. Here we will look at the Bible chronologically, but not from the standpoint of a traditional historical survey. We will focus on the cultural dimensions present in a few key books. This survey is not meant to be exhaustive, but rather suggestive. By focusing on the issue of culture in this way, I do not mean to imply that this is the only, or even the most important, issue in the Bible. But it is a neglected issue to which we need to pay special attention.

Part two then discusses how we can apply in practical ways the biblical teaching on culture to the world today. Chapter eight highlights urbanization as one of the main forces affecting cultures around the world. Chapters nine and ten then cover five main groups on which our evangelism should concentrate, illustrating how to reach each.

Finally, part three discusses the overriding concerns that Christians in any culture should have. Truth and love are seen, in chapter eleven, as the basis for a universal biblical value system. The book closes by looking at the characteristics of true disciples of Christ.

People are different. We can rejoice in our diversity because together we reflect the boundless creativity of our God. We need not fear our diversity because our God is One. The living truth that comes out of diversity is the mystery of his church.

# Part 1

## A Cultural Survey of the Bible

# 2
# Building the Family: Genesis

GENESIS IS THE BOOK of many beginnings—of the world, of humanity, of sin, of reconciliation, of promise. The beginning of culture is here too. And culture, in Genesis, begins with the family. In Genesis God has much to tell us about what the family is and what it should be, even in a cross-cultural setting.

**Both Male and Female**
Genesis 1—2 tells us how God wanted this world to be, in particular, how he wanted us as people to be. Genesis 1:26 reads, "Then God said, 'Let us.' " Immediately we see a hint of the plurality of God. In the New Testament the teaching becomes explicit. God is a triunity—Father, Son and Holy Spirit. This is a mystery, a unique doctrine. But we need to understand this plurality in Genesis because the passage goes on to say, " 'Let us make man in our image, after our likeness; and let them [notice: let *them*] have dominion over

the fish of the sea, and over the birds of the air, and over the cattle, and over all the earth, and over every creeping thing that creeps upon the earth.' So God created man in his own image, in the image of God he created him; male and female he created them" (Gen. 1:26-28).

The nature of man includes both male and female. The Bible often refers to the whole human race as *man,* just as I will. Usually the context makes it very clear if a specific male is being considered. But more often than not, we should assume that when the Bible refers to *man,* it means both male and female.

I did not understand this until I left America for Africa, because probably no society in the world is more individualistic than that in America. When I first held tryouts in Kenya for a track meet, I could not get the students to compete against each other. They said, "We will select the one among us who is the fastest runner. He will run against the other school." I asked, "Why?" They said, "If we pick the one who can run best for us, then we can all cheer him on to victory against the other school. But we could never cheer him on to victory if he had selected himself by his own qualities. If we compete against ourselves, we will divide ourselves, and we will not be able to compete against the other school." That's corporateness. That is the way a tribal society operates. They do not know what it means to be individual. God created us in this kind of corporateness, "male and female he created them."

Genesis 2:18-24 reinforces this concept. Remember that throughout the six days of creation God evaluated his work as being good. Yet suddenly we read, "Then the LORD God said, 'It is not good.' " What is not good? "It is not good that the man should be alone." Maleness is good, but is not good by itself. So he says, "I will make a helper fit for him."

God helps Adam come to the same conclusion through an inductive process. In verse 19 he forms the animals and birds out of the ground and parades them before Adam, instructing him to name them all. In verse 20 Adam looks at each and every one of God's creatures and names them. This demonstrates that from the beginning God created maleness as a complete entity, able to function alone, by itself. Adam had the capacity to commune with God, to exercise some dominion over nature, to be creative in thinking up names. But it was not good that he should be alone. And as he began to function alone, in maleness, he discovered what God already knew—that this was not good. This was made especially vivid as Adam was introduced to every kind of living creature that existed yet found none that was like him. He realized that though he was in complete harmony with nature, there was nothing in nature like him. He was alone, and this was not good.

After God creates Eve, he brings her to Adam, just as God brought the animals. But this time Adam's response is quite different. "This at last is bone of my bones and flesh of my flesh" (2:23). Here is someone like me! This is just what I've been looking for! Adam then gives the woman a name. After looking at every kind of animal on the earth and discovering his uniqueness, now he sees that uniqueness in a mirror image. "Therefore a man leaves his father and his mother and cleaves to his wife, and they become one flesh. And the man and his wife were both naked, and were not ashamed" (2:24). This is what God thought was very good, man in a family which in its unity expresses the nature of God.

**Breakdown Begins, Reconciliation Begins**
In chapter 3 sin enters, and there is an immediate breakdown of the relationships which God has established in his creation. "And they heard the sound of the LORD God walking in the garden in the cool of the day, and the man and his wife hid themselves from the presence of the LORD

God among the trees of the garden" (3:8). The first break-down is that man and woman are alienated from God. They are now hiding from him.

Then, in verse 10 we read, "And he said, 'I heard the sound of thee in the garden, and I was afraid because I was naked; and I hid myself.' " Sin has also broken down man's relationship with himself. He sees himself as inadequate. He is uncomfortable with himself. He is ashamed, and so he hides from God.

We see a third breakdown in verse 12. "The man said, 'The woman whom thou gavest to be with me, she gave me fruit of the tree.'" The relationship between the man and the woman has changed drastically because of sin. This is no longer the rejoicing of "At last . . . bone of my bones and flesh of my flesh." This is tension, alienation, separation. The unity that God intended is gone. The corporateness is gone.

Lastly we come to verse 17. "And to Adam he said, 'Because you have listened to the voice of your wife, and have eaten of the tree of which I commanded you, "You shall not eat of it," cursed is the ground because of you; in toil you shall eat of it all the days of your life.' " No longer will man and woman exercise dominion over nature by working with it but by working against it. They are alienated from creation.

The breakdown of the system moves God to intervene. He takes an immediate step of reconciliation. "The LORD God made for Adam and for his wife garments of skins, and clothed them" (3:21). God reached down in his mercy and acted to rebuild their relationship with him. The man and woman were incapable of taking the initiative here. So God acts on their behalf.

God also acts to rebuild the relationship between man and himself. God helps protect man from man's own self-destructive tendencies. He also puts clothing around man, around woman, to care for their nakedness. In doing this God makes it possible for man to be comfortable with himself, to be in a relationship with himself which he can handle. Underneath, man and woman still have trouble accepting themselves, but God has provided a way so they can at least continue to function in at least a moderately normal fashion.

Then, in 3:22-23 we learn, "The LORD God said, 'Behold, the man has become like one of us, knowing good and evil; and now, lest he put forth his hand and take also of the tree of life, and eat, and live for ever'—therefore the LORD God sent him forth from the garden of Eden, to till the ground from which he was taken." God also protects the man and woman from themselves by putting out of their reach the temptation of taking that second fruit and living in eternal death.

This sending out is not merely a negative act of protection. It is also a positive act of commission. They are sent out for a purpose. They are sent out to till the ground. They are not allowed to sit around and vegetate or degenerate in self-loathing. They are given a task. In the task we see just the beginnings of re-creation or reconciliation between man and creation. It is obviously partial. But it is a foretaste of the full reconciliation God plans.

God then helps rebuild the relationship between man and woman. "Now Adam knew Eve his wife, and she conceived and bore Cain, saying, 'I have gotten a man with the help of the LORD' " (4:1). The sexual relationship between man and woman suddenly takes on a whole new meaning. Before it was part of God's creation, now it is the means by which man and woman who, because of sin need to keep skins on themselves, can now get those skins off and become united again. In other words there is a process by which God instills in man the ability to reunite that maleness and femaleness.

## The Family of Cain

All of this, of course, is not adequate. Man is still alienated from God. Man is still separated from self and from spouse and from creation. God therefore begins a long-term process of reconciliation as he builds family and community.

Genesis 4 concentrates on family, in particular on the family of Cain. But the example is a negative one, showing degeneration within a family rather than upbuilding.

"Now Abel was a keeper of sheep, and Cain a tiller of the ground" (4:2). Anthropologically, this is the basic division of mankind—the farmer versus the herdsman, the migrant tribes versus the stable tribes. Most of the wars of early history were fought between the herdsmen and the farmers. In the United States the homesteaders going out to the West had great battles with the cattlemen.

The same tension existed between Cain and Abel as well. God accepted Abel's sacrifice but refused Cain's (4:4-5). Apparently Abel had offered first fruits ("the firstlings of his flock") while Cain did not (merely bringing "an offering of the fruit of the ground"). Cain withheld from God the first portion while Abel gave it freely. Cain's response is one that psychologists might call misdirected anger. He's mad at God, but he takes it out on Abel. More simply, Cain is jealous of Abel, and so he kills him (4:8).

God responds to this by forcing him to quit farming and become a fugitive (4:11-12). Cain protests, "My punishment is greater than I can bear. Behold, thou has driven me this day away from the ground; and from thy face I shall be hidden; and I shall be a fugitive and a wanderer on the earth, and whoever finds me will slay me" (4:13-14). So the Lord says to him, "Not so! If any one slays Cain, vengeance shall be taken on him sevenfold" (4:15). So God punishes Cain, sending him out to live in fear of having his head bashed in. And God gives him one bit of security. If anybody kills him, there will be vengeance sevenfold.

By the end of Genesis 4 we come to the man who is at least the great-great-great-grandson of Cain, the last of Cain's line mentioned in the Scripture, Lamech. "Lamech said to his wives: 'Adah and Zillah, hear my voice; you wives of Lamech, hearken to what I say; I have slain a man for wounding me, a young man for striking me. If Cain is avenged sevenfold, truly Lamech seventy-sevenfold' " (4:23-24). This is how the line of Cain has degenerated. Kidner puts it this way: "Lamech's taunt-song reveals the swift progress of sin. Where Cain had succumbed to it (7) Lamech exults in it; where Cain had sought protection (14-15) Lamech looks round for provocation: the savage disproportion of killing a mere lad (Hebrew *yeled,* 'child') for a mere wound is the whole point of his boast (cf. 24). On this note of bravado the family disappears from the story."[1] Sin takes its course and the family disintegrates.

**The Family of Seth**
In contrast, the very next verses, 4:25-26, read, "And Adam knew his wife again, and she bore a son and called his name Seth, for she said, 'God has appointed for me another child instead of Abel, for Cain slew him. To Seth also a son was born, and he called his name Enosh. At that time men began to call upon the name of the LORD." In the next few chapters (Genesis 5—7), we find that the line of Seth from time to time falls back and calls on the name of the Lord. We find that his descendant Enoch walked with God. And Enoch's descendant Methusaleh is noted to have had a special relationship with God. Also within the same line, Noah, turns out to be a man righteous in the eyes of God.

In spite of Seth's family, there were other people on the earth who did not follow God. So God annihilated everybody except for one righteous man. But when God said, "I have seen that you are righteous" (7:1), in God's mind that meant Noah and his wife and their sons and their sons' wives. God does not break up families. The righteousness of Noah affects each individual in his family just as Cain's sin affected those in his. God is working through families to rebuild mankind's relationship with him.

Yet by the time we reach Genesis 11, there is another dilemma. "And the LORD came down to see the city and the tower, which the sons of men had built. And the LORD said, 'Behold, they are one people, and they have one language; and this is only the beginning of what they will do; and nothing that they propose to do will now be impossible for them. Come, let us go down, and there confuse their language, that they might not understand one another's speech" (11:5-6). God is saying in effect, "I created human beings to be special. I gave them many gifts, many abilities. When they begin to use those gifts for themselves, however, for their own glory, it is incredible what they can do. But in the end they will self-destruct." So to protect man from himself, once again God intervenes. He scatters them all over the earth.

That is the last time within the book of Genesis that God deals with mankind as a whole. He says, "I am not going to deal with all of mankind anymore. I am going to select a family, Abraham. I am going to bless that family and through him bless all the other families of the earth."

Abraham's family becomes a model for us. We need to look at the rest of Genesis in that light, because God is intervening in human history to establish his ideal of family.

**The Family of Abraham**
The Genesis story progresses through four more sections related to families. In Genesis 12—15, we see the preparation of Abraham's family. God once again calls a family, not just an individual. God tells Abraham to bring himself and all his responsibilities. That includes Terah, his father, who was too old to care for himself (11:31-32). It includes

Lot who was the son of Abraham's dead brother (11:27-28). It includes his wife. And it includes his possessions. Family relationships are not to be broken.

In the next section (Gen. 16—23) the family is established. We have the well-known stories of Ishmael and Isaac, the promised birth of a son and the disbelief that accompanies it. When Isaac is older, God tests Abraham by asking him to sacrifice Isaac. The era ends with the death and burial of Sarah.

Genesis 24—36 covers the extended family of Abraham. It begins with the search for a wife for Isaac. Then we hear about the line of Esau and the line of Jacob; the latter God blesses and the other he does not. These chapters end with the genealogy of Esau, after which we hear nothing more about his family.

The last section is Genesis 37—50. We see the relationships of Jacob and his children and how those children interact as a family. Joseph is sold into slavery in Egypt by his brothers who envy the special treatment their father Jacob is giving their younger brother. Joseph works his way to the top of the Egyptian government and saves that country, as well as his own family, from famine.

We can draw a number of principles from these chapters. First is one I have already referred to: *family relationships are not to be broken.* In fact, God maintains these relationships in order to fulfill the promises he has given. This can be illustrated in Abraham's relationship with Lot.

After Terah dies, Abraham cares for Lot by setting him up with his own section of ground and making sure Lot is able to be self-sustaining (13:2-13). And God promises Abraham that the land he sees around him will be his own (13:14-16), and he commands Abraham, "Arise, walk through the length and the breadth of the land, for I will give it to you" (13:17). This is the Promised Land.

There is only one problem with the Promised Land:

other people happen to live there. There are four kings on one side of the Valley of Siddim and five kings on the other side. The four kings on one side join together and grab up all of the surrounding villages. The other five kings decide they are not going to stand for this, so they go to war to see who will rule. And what about poor Abraham? He is wandering around in the middle of all that, an itinerant.

The four kings win, but they make a mistake in the process. They take Lot (14:1-12). After all these great warlike machinations, the Bible simply says Abraham "routed them and pursued them" (14:15). He wipes out the four kings. This says a great deal about God's concern for Abraham and God's concern for Lot (who is still part of Abraham's family). But it also says to Abraham, "I am going to fulfill my promise to give you this land as you fulfill your responsibilities to your family. Now you can live in this land in peace." We see the same theme in Genesis 37—50. Joseph maintains his relationship with his family despite their hostility, and God uses this to preserve Abraham's line, saving them from the drought.

Many people read the book of Genesis with their twentieth-century morality in mind. But we have to recognize that God plucked out of savage, alienated mankind a family that he chose to redeem. Keeping this in view we can see how God taught Abraham's family a second principle: *the sanctity of marriage*.

Abraham and Sarah's relationship was typical for the culture they came out of. Marriage was important but not sacred. In Genesis 12 the family goes to Egypt because of a famine. So Abraham says to his wife, "I'm sorry about this, Sarah, but you are a beautiful woman, and I'm going to lose my head if I say you are my wife. So let's just say you are my sister. So you'll be on your own. You can do whatever you want." That's how he views his commitment to marriage. That is how his culture views it. But since he does not know any better, God intervenes to teach him something new. God ratifies the sanctity of the sexual relationship in marriage.

After Sarah is accepted into Pharaoh's household, plagues follow, and Pharaoh discovers they are due to Sarah's presence. So Pharaoh sternly rebukes Abraham and drives him right out of the country (12:17-20). Yet Abraham has not yet learned his lesson and tries the same deception with Abimelech when the family travels to Gerar. God then works through another pagan king to teach him the importance of marriage (Gen. 20). Later, in Genesis 26, we find Isaac employing the same deception as his father. And a third time the family of Abraham is rebuked for its low view of marriage (Gen. 26:1-16).

It was a common pattern of the day. If you could not protect yourself, then you had better do whatever you could to save your neck. Three times God intervenes, once in each of the first three sections that I outlined. In the fourth section, however, we find Joseph saying to Potiphar's wife, "I'll go to jail before I'll violate the purity of a marriage relationship." Where did Joseph ever get an idea like that? From God, who had been building that into his family for four generations.

There is another factor accounting for Joseph's reaction. This brings us to the third principle in Genesis 12—50: *the importance of love in family relationships.* Abraham is promised a son. So he waits. And waits. No son. Sarah suggests he have a child by her maid, Hagar. Abraham agrees. But Sarah becomes upset when Hagar starts flaunting the fact that she has conceived and Sarah hasn't. Sarah demands that Hagar be thrown out and again Abraham agrees. He is willing to expel this woman, who carries his son, into the barren desert. Yet God rebukes Abraham again by saving Hagar and her child. God has more concern for them than

Abraham, a fact which is not lost on Abraham (Gen. 16).[2]

By the time he has a son through Sarah, Abraham is desperate. When the son is born, therefore, a whole new relationship develops. He makes a great feast when the child is born. Yet God wants to develop the father-son relationship further. He says to Abraham, "Take your son, your only son Isaac, whom you love." Do you hear the build-up? Abraham is not just to take his son but his only son. And not just his only son but the son he loves, the son who will mean even more to him when this episode is ended. "And go to the land of Moriah, and offer him there as a burnt offering" (Gen. 22:2). Of course God is accomplishing other things as well, but this is, I believe, an important aspect that is often overlooked.

The importance of love in family relationships continues to be built up in Isaac until he marries Rebekah, and he loves her (Gen. 24:67). Remember that Isaac's wedding is arranged for him in contrast to Isaac's son, Jacob, who chooses his own wife on the basis of what he has seen to be so important in his parents' relationship—love. So Jacob endures seven years of labor under Laban so he can marry the girl he loves—Rachel. (And then seven more on top of that after Laban tricks him into marrying Leah first.) Jacob has an emotion in his breast that few others had expressed, an emotion that God has placed in him.[3]

Joseph, Jacob's son, is the result of the family that God has worked in. After four generations Joseph understands the purity of marriage. The biblical pattern is that sin follows to the third generation. It may also take about three generations to develop solid, godly family relationships. Does it happen in a day? Sometimes we think a marriage can become ideal within a few weeks or months. But it's not so. We are dealing with a basic institution that belongs to God and comes from God. He is building it into a means of communicating his personality to those around us.

A fourth principle we can draw from Genesis is what I call *the maintenance of a name,* the continuation of a family, its lineage. These chapters are full of negative examples. First, Lot's daughters decided to commit incest with their father "that we may preserve offspring through our father" (19:32). They bear sons who are the fathers of the Moabite and Ammonite nations, both of whom later lead Israel into idolatry (Num. 25:1-5; 1 Kings 11:5) and harrass Israel throughout the Old Testament period. All of this originates with a case of incest. Another example is the rape of Dinah, Jacob's daughter, which is avenged by the massacre of the offending family (34:1-34). In yet another case Onan refuses to fulfill his duty to carry on his brother's name and so is put to death (38:8-9). Then Judah, Onan's father, goes to a prostitute only to find out it is his daughter-in-law, Tamar. God does not condemn all these, but neither does he sanction them. He allows the norms of the culture to work themselves through. Yet he also allows the contrasting examples to flourish. The line of Abraham, Isaac, Jacob and Joseph, conceived and nurtured in love and fidelity, is preserved and used by God to proclaim his true character.

The fifth and final principle from Genesis regarding families is *the importance of sibling relationships.* As with maintaining a lineage, we find negative examples—Isaac versus Ishmael and Jacob versus Esau. Even in the fourth generation Joseph's brothers are jealous and sell him into slavery after plotting to kill him. But God has finally broken through in the life of Joseph. He does not hold a grudge against his brothers but seeks to preserve them—and even to reunite the whole family under his care and protection in Egypt. Family ties are not to be broken. Through the years God built the family, allowing variations and sinfulness to run their courses, but never changing the ultimate purpose he had in mind. Cultures might change, but God's Word does not.

## The Family Today

The importance of these principles will be seen much more clearly in chapters nine and ten when I discuss two of the key communication networks in our urbanized world—kinship and ethnicity. But allow me to draw a few preliminary conclusions about how the teaching of the book of Genesis on the family affects our witness. As the church, we are to witness to the world in light of the fact that we have a redeemed kinship and a redeemed volunteer association that all can come into if they will submit themselves to the person of Jesus Christ. God communicates himself through redeemed family relationships. The world should see our redeemed relationships, begin to admire them and say they want the same. Our response? "You can have the same if you will submit yourself to Jesus Christ."

Marriage then is a process of glorifying God; dating is a testing of that process and can glorify God as well. A vital part of our dating patterns should be witness as couples. In double-dating with an unsaved couple, for example, you can better express the fullness of God's personality than by a one-on-one friendship alone. Remember, "God created man in his own image, in the image of God he created him; male and female he created them. . . . 'It is not good that the man should be alone' " (Gen. 1:27; 2:18). It is not what we as individuals do so much as how we relate to other people within the body. We witness through the two basic relationships: marriage and the family of God (the church).

If you are single, one way you might develop a witness is in partnership with a Christian family near you. For example, I have seen many families do what individuals could never do on campus. A dormitory dining hall is chaos. Trying to witness in that context is quite a challenge. But invite that same friend into the living room of a friendly Christian family, and you see how different it is. Many Christian families would be glad to have you use their homes as bases for evangelism. You invite your friends to meet a family you know, have them set you up with Coke and cookies, drift out and then let you use the living room. How quickly the conversation will turn. Let your friends see how this Christian family loves each other and loves you, and how you love them. Your friends may well learn to want to be part of that.

If you are from a Christian home, understand its importance in your witness. You are a product of that family. Take your friends home for a weekend and let them see that family. Let them be amazed. We do not realize the gift that we have in Christian homes. After we had been in Reading, Pennsylvania, just eight months, four people on the block asked us, "What is so different about your family?" The doors for witness were wide open.

## God's Time Frame and Ours

Let me conclude this chapter by discussing one important principle in crosscultural witness: *God's time frame is not our time frame.* Satan has tried to have a strong influence in every culture, sometimes with more success than others. So when people become Christians within a culture, they may find that most of what they are doing is at odds with where God is going. One of the common mistakes that missionaries made in the colonial era was to encourage them to change immediately from their cultural patterns to Christian patterns of life. Condemning polygamy, for example, can destroy the family rather than build it as God intends. It can create divorcées who are forced into prostitution as their only form of livelihood. Too often missionaries have cut into a culture with a fixed value system, calling all people to that value system. But God is saying, "I'm going to meet all individuals where they are and begin to work a regenerative process within their lives. And it may take four generations to complete the regeneration as it did with the patriarchs." What missionaries are now learning and applying, we must also apply in other crosscultural ministries.

When Beth (not her real name) was sixteen, she had her first child. By the time she was twenty she had had three children by two different men. She had dropped out of high school. She never went anywhere. Her whole life was messed up. Then she met a Black pastor in Philadelphia who met her where she was and introduced her to the power of the gospel.

But now what? She is on welfare; she has no education; she has three children with no husband; she's living with a man; she's in a Philadelphia Housing Authority house that is a mess; she's living in a neighborhood where her daughter will be pregnant (by force or otherwise) before she is fourteen. That's the nature of the neighborhood. Beth has to have a man in the house if she is going to have protection. That's the nature of the neighborhood too. She's been redeemed. She's been regenerated. But what do you do? Where do you start?

I know what I would like to do—snatch her and her lovely children right out of that nasty environment and put her out in some good, clean place. But reality says you cannot operate that way. So I asked Beth, "Where do you think God is taking you?" It was amazing how God's Spirit gave her insight light years beyond where one would expect.

She put together the following plan. "My daughter is now eleven. Within two years I have got to get her out of this neighborhood. I have no education and no money. But if I get one year of education and take a practical nurse's course, I can get a job that can provide me with enough extra income to put my daughter in a Christian school. There she can get an education and meet friends during the day which will help her learn to live by Christian values

*40*

during off hours. Then if I continue my education, I can become an R.N. and get a better job which will get me enough money to get all of us out of here in four years."

I met Beth when she was halfway through her four-year plan. But it was my hope that she would not have to stay there for the remaining two years. So together we approached the housing authority about getting her into a better neighborhood. My strategy with the city was to say to them, "In the two years since Beth has become a Christian, her lifestyle has significantly changed. She has completed high school and her nursing course while keeping a full-time job. She has gotten her daughter into a Christian school. In two years she has begun to do everything that she hadn't done in the past ten. So it's obvious that here is a woman who has been turned around. Would you respond by getting her better housing?"

Three months and twenty-seven levels of administration later, I finally worked my way through to the woman at the top who said, "No. We won't move her." That looked like the end of the road. But we went back to the church community and said, "You've got to provide housing for this woman. It means that some of you are going to have to sacrifice to put up the money to get a mortgage. But it's the only way we are going to get her out of there." The church responded and bought her a house in Germantown despite the fact that she was, as we would say, living in sin. They recognized that God was doing a work in her and were content to let him continue at his own pace.

As it turns out, of course, Beth was struggling with her living situation at the same time. She had been talking to me a little, knowing that I was a White from suburbia with certain values. "The Bible says that I shouldn't be living with Lou, since I'm not married to him; however, if I don't live with him, I'm in trouble. If Lou moves out, anybody and everybody on the streets would move in. I would be

*41*

raped every night. His being here is a kind of protection."

I responded by saying, "Look, if the Holy Spirit tells you to do something, you do it."

I also got to know Lou. He started sharing with me his dilemma of marrying. Now that she had become, in his words, a church woman, he shouldn't be living in the house with her. But he knew she needed the protection too. So I said, "Look, that's not my business. If she wants you out, she'll tell you."

A couple of years later I met her pastor and asked about Beth and Lou. "You know," he said, "he's coming around. He's going to be a Christian soon. They'll probably end up getting married."

God has a whole different set of values and a whole different time frame from you and me. He's going to fully regenerate both of them. If we had approached that situaion from our moralistic stance of what is right and what is wrong, we would have interfered in God's plan for that family. A book like Genesis can help us gain God's long-range plan for the family, so we can work in concert with him to regenerate what is fallen.

# 3
# The
# Impact
# of a
# Minority:
# Daniel

GOD'S PROMISE TO ABRAHAM was that through his family all nations would be blessed (Gen. 22:18). With Joseph we see the beginning of the fulfillment of this promise. Egypt was saved from drought and famine through Abraham's family. During the next four hundred years the Egyptian people were brought into an understanding of the sovereign God through the Hebrew people. As the nation left Egypt and went on to conquer the Promised Land, the battles they fought were a witness to all nations of God's power.

During the period described in the books of Joshua and Judges, Israel struggled to establish itself in the land. But a problem arose. While God had ordained that the people of God should in time become the kingdom of God, the Israelites had decided that they wanted to become the kingdom of Israel. In the days of Samuel they started saying, "We want a king." God was opposed to the idea. He was to be their king. But the people continued to make the demand. "We want a dynasty. We want a human institution that we can look to, to be proud of, to make us secure." God knew the problems they would face if they followed this path. But as he often does, God allowed his people to make their own choices. And in the process, he still made them into the people of his choosing.

He began by offering them Saul—their choice—who turned out to be a failure. Saul possessed virtually no religious discernment. He did not know the prophet Samuel existed until Saul's own servant told him. And even then Saul did not seek him out for religious reasons but because he thought Samuel might have some magical power to help him find his lost donkeys (1 Sam. 9:5-10). In contrast God then offered the people David—his choice—who was a great success. God took an obscure shepherd with nothing to commend him and made him into a true king and a man after his own heart.

Out of David's kingdom came Solomon. And after that, God no longer was king. The people said, "The king is our ruler." For the next four hundred years God fought with the Old Testament people to recognize God as their king. But they would not. They came to the point of believing that they could not be destroyed. They were God's people and this was God's land, so they could not be beaten. From the time of Adam, the people of God had not been finally defeated. They had come to see themselves as culturally superior instead of as the people of God. God finally had to destroy his own Temple and his own people to get the whole world to be aware of who he truly was.

We come, then, to the book of Daniel with Judah in exile in Babylon. Daniel is probably one of the most abused books in the Bible. Many simply ignore it, choosing to focus on how God brought Israel back out of exile and missing what he did in it. Others see Daniel as a string of fascinating

Sunday-school stories about praying hard and not being burned up or eaten by lions. Still others allegorize the book out of history or see it solely as a prophecy of the future. We fail to see its plain significance: the story of God's people in Babylon and of how God wants to reveal himself to the world.

Each of the first six chapters of Daniel is a separate story with a final concluding paragraph. Rather than concentrating on the stories, however, I will focus on these final verses which give us the thread of continuity through the book.

**Daniel Stands Out**
The first chapter tells of the conquest of Judah and of how a few of the people were brought to Babylon. Among them Daniel was recognized as a leader. He and a few of his countrymen were given some special training by the Babylonians. In Daniel 1:20 we then read this: "And in every matter of wisdom and understanding concerning which the king inquired of them, he found them ten times better than all the magicians and enchanters that were in all his kingdom." The king recognized that Daniel and his friends were exceptionally bright. Why do you suppose this was so?

In the wilderness God had given his people a system of law. When the law was obeyed and the people followed their God, they had inside information on truth—on science, on social institutions, on psychology. The Israelites were not a bunch of ignorant nomads. A powerful military king conquered the nation of Israel and brought the best of the defeated people back. But in every matter of wisdom and understanding the king found them ten times better than the best of Babylon. Why? Daniel was simply being obedient to his culture, the culture that God had given him. In other words, he had developed a biblical way of life. Daniel did not make the same mistake his countrymen had. He did not credit himself or his culture with superiority.

*45*

He credited God. We too must be careful not to confuse the two.

## Daniel's God

Daniel 2 is the story of Nebuchadnezzar's dream of a statue which Daniel interpreted. The king's response is in the last paragraph. "Then King Nebuchadnezzar fell upon his face, and did homage to Daniel, and commanded that an offering and incense be offered up to him. The king said to Daniel, 'Truly, your God is God of gods and Lord of kings, and a revealer of mysteries, for you have been able to reveal this mystery.' Then the king gave Daniel high honors and many great gifts, and made him ruler over the whole province of Babylon, and chief prefect over all the wise men of Babylon. Daniel made request of the king, and he appointed Shadrach, Meshach, and Abednego over the affairs of the province of Babylon; but Daniel remained at the king's court" (2:46-49). In chapter 1 he saw Daniel as a superior man. Now he had seen why Daniel was superior because he had a God that is superior. We should not read too much into this chapter. The king was not yet following God. Nonetheless, God was at work. The king had recognized that Daniel's God was good for Daniel. So he made Daniel a leader.

The third chapter of Daniel explains why we should not read too much into the second chapter. For here we read the story of Nebuchadnezzar ordering everyone to worship the huge gold statue he has made of himself. While he agreed that Daniel's God was a great God, he still saw himself as greater because, after all, he had destroyed the nation of Daniel's God. Anyone who would not worship the statue would be thrown into the fiery furnace. God, however, takes this opportunity to re-establish his claim as the God of the whole earth—despite what people might think because of the destruction of Judah—and, as he had promised to Abraham, to proclaim his sovereignty to all peoples.

As soon as Nebuchadnezzar made his proclamation, what happened? "Therefore at that time certain Chaldeans came forward and maliciously accused the Jews. They said to King Nebuchadnezzar, . . . 'There are certain Jews whom you have appointed over the affairs of the province of Babylon: Shadrach, Meshach, and Abednego. These men, O king, pay no heed to you; they do not serve your gods or worship the golden image which you have set up'" (3:8-9, 12). The Jews had begun to rise to power and the Chaldeans became jealous. It was like any political conflict. If you are on top, people are going to take pot shots at you whether you have done anything wrong or not because they do not want you on top. They want to be on top. Here, however, was a real opportunity for the Chaldeans to make some gains on these upstart Jews. They were ignoring a direct command of the king.

As we know, they were thrown in the furnace but were saved by God. As a result Nebuchadnezzar made another decree recorded at the end of the chapter. "Therefore I make a decree: Any people, nation, or language that speaks anything against the God of Shadrach, Meshach, and Abednego shall be torn limb from limb, and their houses laid in ruins; for there is no other god who is able to deliver in this way" (3:29). That decree went out to every people, nation or language. Abraham was called from among the nations to be a witness to the nations. The people had failed to do this; so God said, "If you won't speak to the nations from Jerusalem, you'll do it from Babylon."

Put yourself into the position of a Jew in Babylon—captured, abused, your land lost, sent some place to work in slavery. All of a sudden the word comes through: The God of the Jews is a powerful God. Anyone who says anything against this God will be torn to pieces. What do the Babylonians do? They turn to the nearest Jew and say, "You'd better tell me everything you can about your God. I don't want to say anything against him—even by mistake! And I don't want you to go around to some of your government friends and say, 'Listen, I think I heard so-and-so say something against my God.' " So instantaneously the Jews, scattered throughout the Babylonian Empire, are conferred with tremendous political power.

Something else happens as well. It quickly becomes apparent who among the Jews really knows God and knows the Law. Those who had been disobedient, who had not learned the Law but had been the fat cows of Bashan enjoying their riches up on the hill are suddenly nothing. But those who do know the Law, who had gone to the Temple school and could teach the Law to the people begin to gain some power and prestige in the land. Through this decree God is calling out for himself a people—those who know the Law.

Critics have disregarded this decree, claiming that it could not have been implemented. Why? Because the Jews were insignificant at the time. The whole point of the book of Daniel thus far has been the exact opposite—the Jews had grown in power. It would in fact be Jews at the top of the government who would implement the edict.

What about at the bottom of the ladder? Remember that Babylon was not a thriving industrial state of the twentieth century. As soon as you were outside the city, life deteriorated quickly. It would be like the remote villages of today's Third World. The real leaders are the small shopkeepers and teachers who read, write and occasionally visit the big city.

Once when I was in such a village in Kenya, I walked into a shop owned by an Indian. The shopkeeper was explaining to an African that the price of sugar suddenly went up because "your government just added a new transport tax." The Indian had just read this in the paper the day before and was interpreting the African's law to the African. What he did not choose to explain was that the tax would not be put into effect for two months and would not affect the price of sugar for four months—if at all!

There is evidence that long before the exile Jewish traders, educators, merchants and soldiers were not only in Babylon but also India and China. "In a thousand and one ways the Jewish people were thrown into daily contact with their environs, and along with his goods the Jew frequently carried his religion."[1]

## Nebuchadnezzar's God

Nebuchadnezzar had come a long way toward God since chapter 1. But notice that his edict in 3:29 is stated negatively: punishment was to be meted out only to those who spoke against God. People were not required to worship God. And not till Daniel 4 do we have any indication that the king himself finally bowed to Yahweh.

The writer in chapter 4 seems so excited that he has to give the end at the beginning. "King Nebuchadnezzar to all peoples, nations, and languages, that dwell in all the earth: Peace be multiplied to you! It has seemed good to me to show signs and wonders that the Most High God has wrought toward me. How great are his signs, how mighty his wonders! His kingdom is an everlasting kingdom, and his dominion is from generation to generation" (4:1-3). Then Nebuchadnezzar proceeds to tell the story of how he was reduced to madness and then returned to his throne by God. In the last verse he concludes, "Now I, Nebuchadnezzar, praise and extol and honor the King of heaven; for all his works are right and his ways are just; and those who walk in pride he is able to abase" (4:37).

The most powerful king of one of the most powerful kingdoms that have ever ruled the earth sent out a decree that everybody should recognize that he, the king, bows to the Lord God Jehovah. A pagan emperor suddenly did what the Hebrews themselves did not: he proclaimed to all nations that God is Lord. The kings of Israel and Judah did not do anything like this king of Babylon. The sovereign God had acted and put his man on the throne. Right under him were men who also worshiped Yahweh. The influence of the Jews was enhanced still further.

This, I feel, also helps explain why the people came out of the exile as monotheists. Before they had played the harlot with any number of gods. Afterward idolatry was no longer a problem for Israel. Synagogues started to pop up all over Babylon, Africa and Asia.[2] Again, in contrast to critics, it is unlikely that a defeated, insignificant minority group could have come out of the exile in such a strong position if the kind of transformation described in Daniel did not occur.

**An Upstart King**
Years pass, perhaps twenty or thirty, during which much of the kingdom has been ruled by Jews. But the author skips all this. Eventually Nabonidus becomes king of Babylon. He was away from the capital on a military campaign against the invading Persians. He had placed his son, Belshazzar, on the throne to rule in his absence on a limited basis. (Although Daniel 5:2 calls Nebuchadnezzar Belshazzar's father, this is probably a general term indicating that Belshazzar was descended from or related to Nebuchadnezzar.) Belshazzar was a young Turk who was a little fed up with all the Jewishness in the country.

The author lands us in Daniel 5 with Belshazzar's feast. It is the end of the empire, seventy years after the destruction of Jerusalem. The historical record is unclear, but we can piece together a probable scenario.

Belshazzar throws a party for all his young friends in the royal household and during the evening asks that the "vessels of gold and of silver which Nebuchadnezzar his father had taken out of the temple in Jerusalem be brought, that the king and his lords, his wives, and his concubines might drink from them" (5:2). He thus abuses these sacred treasures and mocks the decree of Nebuchadnezzar years ago that Yahweh be respected. "They drank wine, and praised the gods of gold and silver, bronze, iron, wood, and stone" (5:4). But on the wall a hand appears that starts writing, and he realizes that this god does not play games (5:5-9). In verse 10 Belshazzar's mother, the queen, enters. She has not been at the banquet (and as we shall see, neither has Daniel) because this is a party for the new breed of rulers. But she approaches her son, the king, respectfully, "O king, live for ever! . . . Let Daniel be called, and he will show the interpretation" (5:10, 12).

Daniel is brought in. His approach is quite different from the queen mother's. "Let your gifts be for yourself, and give your rewards to another" (5:17). Is that a way to talk to a king? The picture painted here is of a young frightened king facing a senior statesman, a retired prime minister, who has had a lot of power in Babylon. Daniel, in fact, still has enough authority and influence and commitment to God to rebuke this upstart king for abusing Yahweh. Belshazzar reverses direction and a "proclamation was made concerning [Daniel], that he should be the third ruler in the kingdom" (5:29). (Belshazzar is only the second ruler.) But it is too late. "That very night Belshazzar the Chaldean king was slain" (5:30). In other words, the proclamation never got out of the room. Why? What happened? The next verse tells us merely that "Darius the Mede received the kingdom, being about sixty-two years old" (5:31).

We can try to piece together what happened. Darius, probably a key general in the army of Cyrus the Persian,[3] had been moving across the plains and had encountered Nabonidus and defeated him. Nabonidus then backed off into a walled city. Darius saw that it would take months to complete the seige and finish off Nabonidus. By that time the people in the capital city would have heard about the defeat of Belshazzar's father. So thinking that surprise was more important than strength, Darius left part of his army to guard Nabonidus and raced across the plains with the rest of his army to the city of Babylon.

History records that the city fell with no resistance or by a surprise attack on the palace, meeting with little resistance.[4] Either case suggests the use of spies which Darius probably had planted months before. He had learned, no doubt, of the strategic role of the Jewish community scattered throughout the empire. He knew the Jews had a major influence on Babylon's economy. He knew Daniel was their leader. If he did not win Daniel over, the Jews might turn against him and his control would be gone. He might have approached Daniel prior to the takeover. Daniel's response? "Belshazzar isn't helping us one bit; in fact, he's against us. If you can guarantee us the same kind of religious and economic and political freedom we had under Nebuchadnezzar, I am willing to help you overthrow the kingdom." Even if Daniel had not been approached beforehand, he certainly was as soon as the kingdom fell. How do we know? Because it was standard procedure to take the heads off of every leader when you conquered a city. That's what happened to Belshazzar. Daniel was not killed, however, because he was needed. Otherwise it would have been a perfect time for a counterrevolution by the nation of Israel with a return to Palestine.

When a general, weakened in battle, has taken over a large kingdom, if there is a second people, a fifth column, inside who counterattack, they can easily obtain their freedom. Darius was a shrewd man. He had been commissioned by Cyrus to put the new government on its feet. He counteracted the possibility of counterrevolution by making Daniel one of the most important leaders of his kingdom (6:2). This alone gives some indication of the extent of the power that Daniel had in that nation and the kind of control that the Jewish people had.

The pattern of Daniel 6 is the same as Daniel 3; only the names have changed. The Persian leaders, jealous of Daniel's power, set a trap for him, forcing him to disobey an edict of Darius which gets Daniel thrown into a den of lions. God rescues Daniel, and "Then King Darius wrote to all the peoples, nations, and languages that dwell in all the earth: 'Peace be multiplied to you. I make a decree, that in all of my royal dominion men tremble and fear before the God of Daniel, for he is the living God, enduring for ever; his kingdom shall never be destroyed, and his dominion shall be to the end' " (6:25-26). God was getting a lot more mileage out of these pagan kings than he did out of his own.

**Two Models of Salt and Light**
What does Daniel mean to us? God has always been a universal God. His people are present throughout the world. They always have been. Abraham wandered around from Mesopotamia to Egypt. He was just one man, but through him the word about God got out to all people. The Jewish people wandered around and did amazing things. Their reputation and God's reputation went out to all people. When they ceased doing that, God changed tactics and scattered them forceably. Through Daniel and other exiles word about God spread to all people.

I get a little troubled when people ask, "What happens to the heathen who don't hear?" While God may be using you and me to bring his Word to a specific people, he has not abandoned the rest. God has used some unique ways many times in history to make sure that people can have access to him. People have always been found guilty of rejecting God because God has not withheld his Word from them. It is harder for some people to get at it than for others. None-theless, God's Word has always been universal (Rom. 1:18-19).

Second, even today the Jewish nation is reflecting a way of life that they learned in Babylon. Since the time of Daniel, there has hardly been a nation on the earth that has not had a handful of Jews that worked their way into the economic and political superstructures of that nation and controlled it to the point that some rulers persecuted them.

Some may question how much power the Jews have had because of a lack of archaeological evidence. But archaeology rarely tells us anything about a minority people living within foreign boundaries. If the whole of America should collapse today and a thousand years from now people come and look at our buildings or read our history books, would they learn much about the 25 million Black people living in our country? Not as much as they should. Much of it is unrecorded. Or would they know the true significance of even the Jewish people who exist within our boundaries? We build buildings that manifest our own culture. So obviously, people would get the impression that mostly White, Anglo-Saxon Protestants lived in this country. When you go back to the Babylonian Empire, you will not find the archaeological traces of the power of Daniel. But there are the other traces that I have mentioned in this chapter. The Jews have always had power beyond their numbers because they learned a style of life that was taught to them by God. And we should learn from them.

Jeremiah has an interesting prophecy which reads, "Thus says the LORD of hosts, the God of Israel, to all the exiles whom I have sent into exile from Jerusalem to Babylon: Build houses and live in them; plant gardens and eat their produce. Take wives and have sons and daughters; take wives for your sons, and give your daughters in marriage, that they may bear sons and daughters; multiply there, and do not decrease. But seek the welfare of the city where I have sent you into exile, and pray to the LORD on its behalf, for in its welfare you will find your welfare" (Jer. 29:4-7). That is the kind of people we should be—spreading all over the world and working our ways into the economic and political structures of every kind of nation and capturing it for Jesus Christ. Not necessarily by becoming the prime minister, but by just being there and having influence. The Jewish model today is still the model that we should follow.

Another equally valid model is that of the Blacks. The Black migrant people cover the entire Atlantic seacoast, from Brazil and Argentina to Jamaica and Nova Scotia, from Iberia to South Africa. They are a people that for over three hundred years have been shifting and drifting around the earth, learning to live as a visible minority in a hostile environment. We need to learn from them what it means to be salt, what it means to hang on when the world is against you. The existence of the Black community against tremendous persecution for over three hundred years and the existence of the Jewish community against tremendous persecution for over two thousand years should teach us something about the kind of life to which Jesus Christ is calling us.

# 4
# The
# Center
# of History:
# Jesus Christ

WHEN THE KINGS OF Israel and Judah, whom God had established, lost sight of the fact that God's message is to all people, God laid them aside. He then re-established himself and the revelation of himself to the world through the Babylonian Empire. It was not the structure, however, that was important, but the people—God's people—who were to go out to all nations. Indeed, the structure of the kingdom of Israel proved to be an impediment which God removed.

In place of the Israelite kings God began to use people we would not call "committed Christians" to spread his name. As noted in the last chapter, some of the Jews carrying that message were probably cynical. Some must have been embarrassed when others came to them and said, "Hey! The king says I better not offend your God. Tell me about him." They might have scratched their heads and thought, "Well, I should have paid more attention in Temple school. I really don't know very much about my own God. But I know a few things." They at least knew enough to say that the Lord God is One; the Lord God is righteous; and the Lord God must be worshiped. This was not the whole message of redemption. But it was what we could call pre-evangelism. It was preparing the whole world to receive the message of redemption, to receive the Messiah himself.

**Prepare the Way**

Another group of unlikely missionaries, as we also began to see in chapter three, completed the preparation. To look at this group more closely, let's first go back and consider in more detail the second chapter of Daniel.

Nebuchadnezzar had a vision of a giant with a gold head, a silver breast and arms, a brass midsection, and iron legs with feet that were iron mixed with clay. Daniel then interpreted this dream. "You, O king, the king of kings, to whom the God of heaven has given the kingdom, the power, and the might, and the glory, and into whose hand he has given, wherever they dwell, the sons of men, the beasts of the field, and the birds of the air, making you rule over them all—you are the head of gold" (2:37-38). Note that it says, "wherever they dwell . . . you rule." God's message went out to *all* people via Nebuchadnezzar. There was no question about the interpretation. Babylon was the head of gold. Then Daniel says, "After you shall arise another kingdom inferior to you, and yet a third kingdom of bronze, which shall rule over all the earth. And there shall be a fourth kingdom, strong as iron. . . . Just as you saw . . . a stone was cut from a mountain by no human hand, and that it broke in pieces the iron, the bronze, the clay, the silver, and the gold: A great God has made known to the king what shall be hereafter" (2:39-40, 45).

This vision of the statue is about four kingdoms which will ultimately be destroyed when a stone carved without hands hits the feet and topples the whole structure. Then that stone will grow into a kingdom that "shall stand for ever" (2:44). After Babylon, the first kingdom, was the Medo-Persian Empire; following that was the Grecian Empire established by Alexander the Great; after that was the Roman Empire which was supplanted by the Church of Jesus Christ—the Stone.

How was the stage set for Christ? First, as we saw in chapter three, Babylon was used by God to proclaim his word. Daniel was the prime minister of Babylon. Second, Daniel also became the prime minister of the Medo-Persian Empire. This pattern continued with Ezra and Nehemiah, both high officers in the Persian government, who solicited and received help from the Empire to rebuild the walls and the Temple of Jerusalem.

In the book of Esther we also see how God preserved his people despite the plotting of Haman, a jealous rival of the powerful Jews in Persia. In the end Haman hangs from the gallows, a Jew is queen (Esther), a Jew is prime minister (Mordecai) and all the Jews are getting special privileges from the king.

Not only the Persian Empire, but the Greek Empire begun by Alexander continued this practice of granting the Jews within their borders special rights. DeRidder writes, "The Greek world also granted a special status to the Jew, although (1) this was not uniform and the extent of the Jews' rights depended on when, how and for what purpose they came to a given community outside Palestine, (2) the organized Jewish community as a whole stood juridically outside the Greek city and the Jews who lived in it had no civil rights there, (3) isolated Jews could acquire civil rights individually. The focus of Jewish life in the Diaspora must be found in the privileges of the Jewish communities, not in citizen rights in Greek towns."[1]

Rome was purely and simply iron, a military force covering the earth, that had no ultimate commitment to a religious system. Consequently, it was perfectly all right for Jews to continue the process which was begun in Babylon. "In 161 B.C. the Jews had received the status of *peregrini* in the Roman Empire, enabling them to be judged by their own laws and follow their own customs in marriage and inheritance. In 110 B.C. this status was secured for Jews everywhere in all states and kingdoms controlled by or allied with Rome. . . . It was Julius Caesar who said that 'Jews might live according to their Torah,' implying two things: (1) recognition of the Torah as part of the public law of the Empire, and (2) acceptance of any Jewish community anywhere within the Empire as part of a single Jewish people. This was a unique concession."[2] Nestled in the heart of every community across the Roman Empire was a small group of Jews who were highly missionary in their attitude—proselytizing people, establishing synagogues—out of which came the whole Hellenistic (that is, Greek-speaking) Jewish movement.

It has been estimated that at the time of Christ one-tenth of the Roman Empire was Jewish. Two and one-half million lived in Palestine, but possibly twice that number were scattered elsewhere. There were a hundred thousand Jews in Cyrenaica, a million in Egypt, a million in Mesopotamia, a million in Asia Minor and a hundred thousand Jews in Italy.[3] There were Jewish communities in China, India, Europe, Ethiopia and along trade routes that covered Africa south of the Sahara. These offered Christian apostles an open door into virtually every area of the world.

Thomas likely went to India. The Ethiopian eunuch went to his home in North Africa. Paul went to Asia, Macedonia, Greece and Rome. The Hellinists who heard the gospel on Pentecost split to the four corners of the earth. The church has been universal from the beginning.

The meaning of all this is clear. God said through Daniel

that he intended to set up four kingdoms to prepare the world for Christ. By the time Rome was established, the situation was unique in history for the rapid spread of the gospel.

Rome had one language, one system of roads, one system of law maintaining peace under one huge army that had all people under its control. The roads of Rome went from the Himalayas to Spain and from Persia to the coast of North Africa. The speed with which the Roman soldiers were able to move was phenomenal. But the speed with which the gospel was able to move was more phenomenal.

God had prepared the world logistically to communicate his message further and more rapidly then than at any other previous time. And it was into the center of that Empire, the geographic center, Palestine, that God sent his Son.

Let us consider the factors in Christ's life that are important for our discussion of crosscultural ministry.

**Christ the Message**
Paul puts the first factor this way. "He [God] has made known to us in all wisdom and insight the mystery of his will, according to his purpose which he set forth in Christ as a plan for the fulness of time, to unite all things in him, things in heaven and things on earth. In him, according to the purpose of him who accomplishes all things according to the counsel of his will, we who first hoped in Christ have been destined and appointed to live for the praise of his glory" (Eph. 1:9-12). That is what missions is all about. The messengers are those who glorify Jesus. Jesus himself did not come merely to communicate the message. He *is* the message.

We should be careful not to just analyze the life of Jesus Christ to find out how to do missions. He was not here primarily to teach us or merely to demonstrate how to present the message. He is the incarnation of the message of redemption. He came to restore the broken relationships we discussed in chapter two. He lived this message in each area.

First, he lived a fully harmonious relationship to his Father. He prayed regularly to his Father. He taught, "I and the Father are one.... If you had known me, you would have known my Father also; henceforth you know him and have seen him" (Jn. 10:30; 14:7). His life and his death exemplified this unity with the Father which Adam broke. Christ was "obedient unto death" (Phil. 2:8) despite his desire that it not be so.

Second, he lived a fully harmonious life in relationship to himself. Jesus Christ was not an ambivalent person. He did not have inner doubts or confusion. He spoke with authority (Mk. 1:27; Mt. 7:28-29). He had a tremendous singleness of purpose and certainty about his mission (Lk. 4:16-21). He was here to do the will of his Father (Jn. 5:19). He demonstrated what a redeemed life is like.

Third, Christ, through his relationship as Son to his Father, incarnates for us a living model of redeemed family relationships. He was the beloved Son in whom the Father was well pleased. He also demonstrated redemption in marriage, although he was never married, through his husband-like relationship to the church.

In Ephesians 5 Paul says, "Be subject to one another out of reverence for Christ" (5:21). The theme is Christian subjection of one to another. Paul goes on to say that there are two models for this: the church and marriage. "Be subject to one another out of reverence for Christ. Wives, be subject to your husbands [in marriage] as to the Lord [in the church]. For the husband is the head of the wife [in marriage] as Christ is the head of the church, his body, and is himself its Savior" (5:22-23). This pattern continues for the next several verses. We understand what marriage is all about because we have seen Christ's relationship to the church.[4]

Christ built a community based on reconciliation. He unified the oddest assortment of disciples that you could imagine—intellectuals, nonintellectuals, wealthy, poor. Matthew, the tax collector, was a reprobate. He had sold himself out to the Roman system. On the other side was Simon the Zealot, a guerrilla dedicated to the destruction of Rome, a man who not only hated the Romans but who hated every Jew who sold himself to the Roman system. How did Simon the Zealot and Matthew the Traitor come together and form a community? Certainly there was conflict between them. Jesus Christ demonstrated the redemption of community by building reconciliation that superseded individual wants and concerns. Marriage is also a community based on reconciliation. It does not accuse ("that woman you gave me") but forgives and binds together in love (Gen. 4:1).

Finally, Christ lived in harmony and had dominion over his environment. The miracles proved that he had rule over disease (Mk. 1:31-34), over nature (Mk. 4:35-41) and even over death (Jn. 11:1-44). He did not have to hurry from one sick person to another, afraid he would not make it in time to do any good (Lk. 8:40-56). He had dominion over the world around him. We hear a tremendous amount from psychology about the effect and even the control that environment has on people. But Jesus Christ has redeemed us in such a way that we do not *have* to be controlled by our environment.

In summary, the first factor in Christ's life with important implications for crosscultural ministry is the way he lived the message of redemption. We too are called not merely to tell others about the gospel but to live it before them as well. We are to live in harmony with God, with ourselves, with others and with our environment.

## A Cosmic Cultural Barrier

Another factor important to crosscultural ministry is the Incarnation, the full humanity which Christ took on. Paul writes, "Christ Jesus, . . . though he was in the form of God, did not count equality with God a thing to be grasped, but emptied himself, taking the form of a servant, being born in the likeness of men" (Phil. 2:5-7). Jesus is fully God. Yet he chose to set aside the cloak of deity and become fully human. He crossed a cosmic cultural barrier. He identified totally with those he came to minister to and left behind his divine heritage.

Jesus chose willingly to accept the limitations of his adopted culture. Under Roman rule, his family was forced by the government to leave their home to go pay taxes in Bethlehem, where he was born. A mad king wanted to kill him, so once more the family was uprooted, and he was carried as an infant to Africa where he spent the first years of his life. Later, they moved back to a small area of Palestine where Jesus became a village carpenter, a role of low social standing. He was of a royal line, but his family was quite poor.

We are often concerned about the limitations a culture might place on us—fewer Christians to gain support from, fewer Christian books in the native language, less money, fewer physical comforts, greater governmental restrictions. Christ accepted all these limitations and more.

Why should the King of Glory reject all his power and wealth? Why should he accept restrictions of time, space, humanness and culture? Why shouldn't he openly proclaim himself as God and present the simple truth of salvation? To answer these questions let us first look at the temptations of Christ in the desert.

Jesus has been fasting for forty days and is hungry. So the Tempter comes along with the first temptation and says, "If you are the Son of God, command these stones to become loaves of bread." Satan challenges Jesus' divinity. "If you are the Son of God, then prove it by doing a miracle. Turn these rocks into stone. Show us you've got divine power." But Jesus refuses and answers, "It is written, 'Man shall not live by bread alone, but by every word that proceeds from the mouth of God" (Mt. 4:3-4). Notice, "*man shall not live by bread alone.*" He does not appeal to any powers or abilities beyond the accepted limitations of humanity.

Again Satan tempts Jesus to perform (almost like a circus high-dive act) another miracle: "Throw yourself down from the top of the temple and let the angels catch you." Once more Jesus could have drawn on any resource to combat Satan, but he stayed within the bounds of what is available to us. "The Scripture says we are not to tempt God. We are not to try to make him perform miracles like a trained animal to increase our faith."

Lastly Satan decides to match his great power and wealth against that of a seemingly destitute God. "I will give you all the kingdoms of the earth if you will worship me." Satan says he will give these to us as well if we will give him the one thing he requires. Jesus rebukes Satan as we can, without an appeal to divine power. "It is written, 'You shall worship the Lord your God and him only shall you serve" (Mt. 4:10).

This also offers us hope as we cross cultures. We can accept what may seem to be tremendous limitations from other cultures and still live a life of full obedience to God. As I said earlier, Christ was not controlled by his environment. He willingly submitted to certain restrictions and yet overcame them to accomplish his mission. If the limitations are human, we too can supersede them as humans. "For as by a man came death, by a man has come also the resurrection of the dead. For as in Adam all die, so also in Christ shall all be made alive" (1 Cor. 15:21-22). Through Jesus' conquest of sin and death, we too can be conquerors in life.

*65*

## Beyond Human Limits

Not only *can* we take part in Christ's victory, it is God's plan from eternity that we should. As I quoted Ephesians 1 earlier, God intends to unite all things in Christ. How? "In him [Christ], according to the purpose of him [God] who accomplishes all things according to the counsel of his will, we who first hoped in Christ have been destined and appointed to live for the praise of his glory" (Eph. 1:11-12). God plans to fulfill his plan through us! As Paul writes later in the book, "The plan . . . [is] that through the church the manifold wisdom of God might now be made known" (Eph. 3:9-10).

This is why I believe that Christ did not come primarily as an evangelist. If he had, he certainly would not have passed by all the people he did and he would have presented a much more straightforward message. Unlike many Jews he did not make proselytes and bring people into a Jewish setting. Instead, he came to reveal the kingdom of God, to build a community. He developed a small group of people who lived with him and ate with him and talked with him. Even in the upper room (Jn. 14) he was still teaching them, and they still did not understand. But he would not give up on them despite this, despite the betrayal of one of the inner circle and despite his impending death.

Eventually, it became necessary for Jesus to return to his Father so his church remaining here on earth could fulfill its task. Jesus did this in order to send the Spirit to take up residence in all his followers. Now in and through us he is able to be young and old, rich and poor, educated and uneducated, Black, Yellow, Red and White. As a body, we now can overcome all limitations of time, space, humanness and culture. Let us live to the praise of his glory.

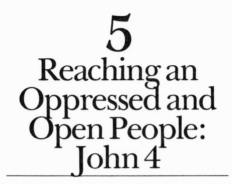

# 5
# Reaching an Oppressed and Open People: John 4

AFRICANS ARE ESSENTIALLY a proverbial people, a people who talk in proverbs. So the Scripture often means much more to them than to us because even Jesus Christ taught in proverbs. When I was a missionary in Africa, the Africans pointed out to me that anybody who teaches in proverbs also talks in proverbs. Proverbs in Scripture are not only found in the specific parables that Jesus taught, but also in the way Scripture itself is put together.

People who think in proverbs or parables often view history differently than we do. We think history is this event and that event strung like beads on the string of time. But all historians know that mere chronology is not history. Our opinions, our biases, our humanness skew or distort history.

Africans recognize from the beginning that history embodies truths which are far more important than the mere recording of facts. They also know that stories convey meaning in life-giving ways that far exceeds a list of principles. It surprised me how much truth in Scripture is conveyed in just this way. The story of the Samaritan woman in John 4 is one such story. It is truth about life embedded in history.

The key to understanding John 4 is parallel thinking. A parable begins with two lines of parallel thought. For example, we might start talking about the consequences of overconfidence and tell the story of the tortoise and the hare. Immediately people are transferring the story into their real experience as it is being told. At the end, of course, the storyteller will explicitly tie the two together and make an application. "Like the hare, you could lose the football game tomorrow if you are overconfident." John 4 is, of course, more complex than that, but the principle holds.

**Through the Ghetto**
As the chapter opens, Jesus is in Judea, antagonizing the Pharisees because of his success in making disciples. He knows his time has not yet come, so he decides to go north to Galilee and let things around Jerusalem cool off for a while. The quickest way to Galilee from Judea was through Samaria. But most Jews insisted on making the trip by going the long way around the east side of the Dead Sea. They felt Samaritans were semipagan, semicivilized half-breeds. They would make themselves religiously unclean if they had anything to do with these people. And besides that—it was dangerous!

Samaria was like a ghetto. No one likes to go through someone else's ghetto. It makes us uncomfortable because the people there are different—not worse, just different. We develop myths about the ghetto to justify our actions. "Everybody that goes there gets mugged." The Jews had created the same myth about Samaria because, being

cultural beings like ourselves, they did not like to be some-
place that is culturally different. This is a form of ethnocentricity, the belief that your people are the good people—
the best people—and no one else matches up.

Jesus, however, "had to pass through Samaria" (v. 4).
Now the heat might have been on from the Pharisees, and
he had to get out of town as quickly as possible. But Jesus
also had to be consistent with truth. If he had accepted the
ethnocentricity that rejected the Samaritans, he would not
be consistent with who he was. It was indeed necessary
for him to go the direct route, right through the heart of
Samaria.

He came to a town in Samaria called Sychar with a well
and a field that once belonged to the patriarch Jacob who
later gave them to Joseph's family (v. 5; see Josh. 24:32). We
have a true story in a historical context about a real place.
It reminds us that the Samaritans and the Jews have a common past. They both claimed Jacob as their father. There is
a basis here for communication. This fact is ignored by the
Jews, but not by the narrator.

In verse 6 we are told that "Jesus, wearied as he was
with his journey, sat down beside the well." Perhaps Jesus
wanted to test his disciples and said, "I'm tired and want
to rest a while. Why don't you get us something to eat in
town?" Or it might have been that Jesus said, "We're all
tired; let's sit down," but the disciples responded, "No,
we're not too tired. We think we'll check out the town." In
either case, they probably had the wrong attitude. It may
have been necessary for Jesus to go through Samaria, but
it wasn't for them.

## The Well and the Town

This is where the two parallel lines begin. "There came a
woman of Samaria to draw water. Jesus said to her, 'Give
me a drink.' " This is immediately followed by, "For his

disciples had gone away into the city to buy food" (vv. 7-8). Jesus is at the well. The disciples are in the town. In both cases we have a confrontation between Jew and Samaritan. John 4 only gives details of one of these stories, assuming readers will draw parallels to the other story on their own. Let me make some of the parallels explicit.

Jesus is at the well asking the Samaritan woman for a drink. Apparently the disciples are in the town asking some Samaritan vendors for food.

The woman responds to Jesus, "How is it that you, a Jew, ask a drink of me, a woman of Samaria?" (v. 9). How do the Samaritans in town respond to the disciples? Imagine twelve big, bearded Black men walking up the street of a modern, White, suburban community. Some residents will call the police, some will say, "May I help you?" and some will just peek out of their windows. Or reverse the situation. What if twelve White police officers start strolling down a Puerto Rican neighborhood? How will the residents react? They will have the same kind of suspicion and curiosity and concern that the woman expresses. It's a human reaction regardless of time and place.

Jesus answers, "If you knew the gift of God, and who it is that is saying to you, 'Give me a drink,' you would have asked him, and he would have given you living water" (4:10). He asks for water but says living water is what matters. The disciples might have done the same, though they didn't. They could have gone into town looking for bread and telling people about the bread of life. "The bread of life is waiting for you just outside the gates. There's no way we would have come here on our own. You're right. Jews and Samaritans don't get along. But this man out there is changing our lives—and everyone else's too." Yet nothing like this happened.

Out at the well the woman responds, " 'Sir, you have nothing to draw with, and the well is deep; where do you get that living water? Are you greater than our father Jacob, who gave us the well, and drank from it himself, and his sons, and his cattle?' Jesus said to her, 'Every one who drinks of this water will thirst again, but whoever drinks of the water that I shall give him will never thirst; the water that I shall give him will become in him a spring of water welling up to eternal life' " (4:11-14). He is raising her consciousness of spiritual truth and rousing her curiosity and interest.

"The woman said to him, 'Sir, give me this water, that I may not thirst, nor come here to draw.' Jesus said to her, 'Go, call your husband, and come here' " (4:15-16). The hour is noon. No one is around but the two of them. In the hot Middle East, the time to go to the well is in the cool of the morning or the evening. It is a social time as well when women talk and children play. Those who come to the well at other times are those who do not want to be at or who are not welcome at such gatherings; that is, the outcasts, the cripples, the disreputable. The woman is not sick nor crippled. Neither does she want total solitude since she's willing to converse with a man sitting alone at the well. This is a disreputable woman cast out by society. She could be a prostitute, a woman of the street. Jesus, of course, perceives her social standing and reputation. This does not bother him at all, however. Indeed, he even begins to broach this most sensitive area of her life, her point of greatest need, because he is concerned about her as a person and not about how uncomfortable it might be to discuss such things with such a person.

How many of us have thought of going to certain sections of town to witness to prostitutes? These women are in a cultural group that has been totally rejected by many Christians. Fear jumps inside us when we even think of meeting them. "Oh, what would my fellow Christians say?" Many Jews had quite a lot to say about Jesus hanging around with publicans and sinners. They even called him a drunkard because of the people he associated with (Mt. 11:19). That did not stop Jesus from having daily contact with them. But it stops us.

Others, however, will object, "But you don't want to put yourself in a place of temptation!" Yet if our commitment to God is so low that in the process of serving him we can be sidetracked easily by a woman on the street, then we probably need to examine whether our faith is true or not. Has it really changed us? Has it given us power or not?

These excuses, these fears, keep us from seeing that these women are lonely and in tremendous need. They are often very willing to engage in serious conversation. At the beginning they will assume that a man's interest is purely motivated by business. It will take a little time before they realize you have other things on your mind. Jesus likewise allows time to converse, even about "business" matters. "Go, call your husband, and come here," he says (v. 16). This may have been a prophetic statement about the woman's marital status, but it might also easily be interpreted as a way for this potential customer to find out if she really was a prostitute. And she says, "I have no husband" (v. 17), which is a way of saying, "Yes, I'm available."

All this would be quite normal for a man and a woman conversing at the well at noon until Jesus' next comment: " 'You are right in saying, "I have no husband"; for you have had five husbands, and he whom you now have is not your husband; this you said truly.' The woman said to him, 'Sir, I perceive that you are a prophet'" (vv. 17-19). The woman now realizes, "He's not interested in business. He's interested in me as a person and wants to talk about important things. He knows my reputation and isn't repulsed. He wants to discuss spiritual truth with me." So she goes on to say, "Our fathers worshiped on this mountain; and you say that in Jerusalem is the place where men ought to worship" (v. 20).

A prostitute in our society might say, "You know, if I ever went to your church, I'd be thrown right out." And I would have to say, "You're right." In a way, Jesus does too. But he is not daunted and moves on. "Woman, believe me, the hour is coming when neither on this mountain nor in Jerusalem will you worship the Father. You worship what you do not know; we worship what we know, for salvation is from the Jews. But the hour is coming, and now is, when the true worshipers will worship the Father in spirit and truth, for such the Father seeks to worship him" (vv. 21-23).

In effect he says, "I'm a Jew, yes. And I know Jews have been keeping you out of Jerusalem. I also know truth is in Jerusalem with the Jews. Because you Samaritans don't come to Jerusalem, you don't have all the truth you could have. You worship in ignorance. But soon it won't matter where you worship. In fact, you can worship God right here and now because God's only requirement is that you worship in spirit and truth."

## When Two Cultures Meet

Jesus has overcome two of the great difficulties inherent in crosscultural witness. First is the problem we have in speaking. There comes a time in our witness to those in other cultures when we have to honestly acknowledge our own background. Indeed, we must accept our own heritage—its good points and its bad—before we can gain a hearing. The danger exists that we might unconsciously present the gospel with our cultural accretions dominating rather than being submitted to God's truth. This can be overcome, though, if we know our own heritage (Black, White, Hispanic, Chinese, Polish, Italian, Indian, whatever) and understand how it affects our Christianity as well as our communication with others. It is apparent that Jesus has come to terms with his background, both in its positive and negative aspects.

The second problem Jesus has overcome is that of our audience's ability to listen. Let's say you are a White Christian who approaches a Black person. Without saying a word you have automatically communicated something about your Christianity which makes it difficult for a Black person to listen to you. You may not like it, but it is a fact that Blacks will associate your Christianity with the maintenance of slavery and of a social system that oppresses people. Christianity has been one of the big whips used to lash the back of the Black community in America. You, as a White Christian, are therefore the enemy.

How can we deal with this? It is the same problem as a Jew saying, "I want to share the truth with you," and a Samaritan responding, "Who says! You've had the so-called truth all these years and wouldn't let us be part of it. What's so different now?"

Jesus acknowledges that this debate has raged and that his culture is in error. It is not important where one worships. What is important is truth and how we respond to it. Great things are about to happen in this regard, he says. In fact, they have already started.

The woman then responds, "I know that Messiah is coming (he who is called Christ); when he comes, he will show us all things" (v. 25). This Samaritan woman who had been rejected by the Jewish system is still willing to buy the notion of a coming Messiah. Jesus takes this hint of openness and runs with it. "I who speak to you am he" (v. 26).

How often do we respond instead like the disciples may have? In town they probably said, "We want some bread," to which the baker might have replied, "What would Jews want to buy bread from Samaritans for?" "Just shut up and give us some bread, half-breed." The conversation would no doubt have ended there.

Whatever happened in town, you can see the rejection the disciples exude when they return from this town trip. "They marveled that he was talking with a woman, but none said, 'What do you wish?' or 'Why are you talking with her?' " (v. 27). They are afraid to ask Jesus these questions. The woman picks up their racism and recognizes that Jesus is in an awkward situation. But he continues to identify with her, as socially unacceptable as she is. He does not break off the conversation. But she is getting uncomfortable enough that she decides this might be a good time to leave, at least for the moment. You see, she does not bring her water jar along, indicating that she intends to come back to get it and continue her talk with Jesus.

**The Ripe Fields**
At this point in the story the two parallel lines of the parable shift. While the story in view was Jesus and the woman, now it is Jesus and the disciples. And while the parallel story was the disciples and the townspeople, now it is the woman and the townspeople.

The disciples begin, " 'Rabbi, eat.' But he said to them, 'I have food to eat of which you do not know.' So the disciples said to one another, 'Has any one brought him food?' Jesus said to them, 'My food is to do the will of him who sent me, and to accomplish his work' " (vv. 31-34). He rejects the food they probably obtained in an ungodly manner and says, "There is something more important in this world than food. But you've been more concerned with eating than with doing God's will."

Jesus goes on to make his point more clearly. "Do you not say, 'There are yet four months, then comes the harvest'? I tell you, lift up your eyes, and see how the fields are already white for harvest" (v. 35). The scene is Jesus sitting with his disciples just outside the village. He gestures toward the gates of the town and says, "Lift up your eyes," as the woman and a group of townspeople begin to emerge. "I sent you to reap that for which you did not labor; others have labored, and you have entered into their labor" (v. 38). He is rebuking the disciples. "The same people you passed by, ignored or snubbed were ready to respond to the good news. I sent you into town to share the truth with them. But you walked right through a ripe field and didn't even know it was ready to be harvested. I've had a short conversation with a woman who is an outcast even in her home town. But she's in there telling them about me, and they're responding. They want to know more."

"Many Samaritans from that city believed in him because of the woman's testimony, 'He told me all that I ever did.' So when the Samaritans came to him, they asked him to stay with them; and he stayed there two days. And many more believed because of his word. They said to the woman, 'It is no longer because of your words that we believe, for we have heard for ourselves, and we know that this is indeed the Savior of the world'" (vv. 39-42). They believed first because of the words of the woman and then because of the words of Jesus. Significantly the words of the disciples are absent. They played no part in this evangelism. If the disciples had expressed any concern to the Samaritans, any compassion, any hint that there was a man out at the well who was concerned about them and their spiritual condition, the Samaritans would have responded. But the disciples rejected their relationship with Jesus and chose not to get involved.

### Who Sowed the Seed?
Jesus told them, "For here the saying holds true, 'One sows and another reaps.' I sent you to reap that for which you did not labor; others have labored" (vv. 37-38). Who had been sowing the seeds of the gospel in Sychar? Not the Jews. They rejected Samaritans. Not Jesus. He had not been

there before. Certainly not the disciples. Who was it then?

God, in his concern for all people, has allowed truth to infiltrate every culture. In particular, the Samaritans had a culture that identified with Jacob and the well and with much Old Testament law. While they had many gaps in their theology, much truth had already been sown in their midst, and they were ready to receive more.

God has done the same thing within other culture groups in our country and around the world. The Black community in America is one such group. When Blacks were first brought to this country, slave masters used Christianity as a tool to maintain a submissive spirit among the slaves. But God had planted the seed, and he used this evil practice for good. Out of slavery came a vibrant Black church.

Today many White Christians in this country believe that the Black church needs to come to Jerusalem—out in the suburbs. We say that the Blacks, like the Samaritans, have been cut off from the truth, thus they hold only a partial gospel. "After all," we say, "The Black church has a rather emotional gospel. That is only part of the story." The irony is that while many of us believe that we possess the whole truth which Blacks need, we will not allow them to join in our fellowship despite their efforts to do so.

The irony does not end there, for we are wrong in think- ing that Jerusalem is in the suburbs, in the middle-class mentality. The White church, too, needs to come to the true Jerusalem—we have not yet arrived. We, too, hold only a partial understanding of the truth. Certainly we have abso- lute truth in God's Word, but we do not have exhaustive or total truth in the Bible or in our understanding. If all people—Black, White, Hispanic, Asian—will share the par- tial truth we each have, then we will all have a more com- plete picture.

There are many culture groups who have the seeds of truth. They are fully ripe for the harvest. We can join that harvest if we will be compassionate, sensitive and humble. Our task is to discover what truth God has already given to a people, emphasize that, and lay aside cultural differences. Jesus says, "The issue is not Jerusalem. In fact, I just came out of Jerusalem, and they don't accept me either. Let's talk together about God and his truth and how we can have greater access to him." We should not arrogantly assume that we have all the truth and that it is our God-ordained duty to enlighten the ignorant everywhere. Nor should we reject people and refuse to have contact with them because we feel they are inferior. Rather, by God's grace, after the example of Christ, let us go in humility and love to the harvest he has prepared.

# 6
# Dividing Power, Multiplying Disciples: Acts (Part One)

A KEY GOAL OF GOD'S PEOPLE on earth is oneness in Christ. We all want unity in truth and love—as long as it is unity on *my* terms. Many Christians, especially in America, believe that in Christ all our differences should disappear. We should think alike, act alike, feel alike. This belief is tied to the myth of the Great American Melting Pot in which everyone becomes part of one uniform identity. Our tolerance for diversity is therefore often quite low. If some people do not have exactly the same theology or order of worship or type of music, or the same views on the military or homosexuality, then they may not be Christian at all, we say.

"Why can't we be like the New Testament church?" some ask. "After all, they were all united. They lived together in brotherhood and peace. The church was truly one then, as God intended. Why can't we be like that now?" The early church was unified, but it was not uniform. And there was brotherhood, but not without struggle and misunderstanding. Yet the book of Acts as it actually stands is more helpful to us than if it merely presented an idealized church. It shows us how by the Spirit we can come to terms with cultural differences and work through resulting tensions.

## A Division among the Jews

As I mentioned in chapter four, Jews were to be found in significant numbers throughout the Roman Empire as well as in Africa, India and even China. This was known as the Diaspora or the Dispersion of the Jews. Jerusalem remained, to a great extent, the focus of the Jewish religion, as well as an international center of trade. Some Diaspora Jews took on many of the customs of those they lived among. Hellenists (Jews influenced by the Greek culture, speaking the Greek language) probably constituted the largest subgroup within the Diaspora. There were also Mesopotamian Jews, Egyptian Jews, Asian Jews and others.

Some of the Diaspora Jews, however, did not accommodate to their surrounding context. They held steadfastly to their own culture, traditions and language (Aramaic). This united them with like-minded Jews who predominated in Palestine (Judea and Galilee). These Palestinian Jews, as I call them, considered themselves superior to other Jews because of their association with the traditional land of King David dominated by the Holy City of Jerusalem. The Pharisees, who epitomized this group, held to what they felt was the purest form of Judaism. Hellenistic Jews, for example, would still consider Judaism superior, but they were more open to other peoples, more "missionary-minded" and prepared to accept proselytes than Palestinian Jews.

Among the Hellenists the synagogue, which developed after the Babylonian exile, was often a center for Jewish evangelism, especially when services were conducted in Greek. The Jewish monotheism, moral values and way of

*80*

life appealed to Gentiles who underwent instruction, circumcision and baptism. Nonetheless it could take two or three generations to become fully identified as a Jew. Thus, even in Jerusalem, synagogues developed around language groups, cultures, classes and even trades.

Many Gentiles, repulsed by the requirement of circumcision, would not become full proselytes (though they might have their sons circumcised). Instead these so-called God-fearers would hang around the edges of Judaism, learn from it and support it. Cornelius (Acts 10:1-2), whom I will consider more in the next chapter, was one such man, as was the centurion with the sick slave whose faith Jesus commended (Lk. 7:1-10).

Thus tension arose among the Jews, especially among the different groups living in and around Jerusalem. To summarize this pecking order, Palestinian Jews were on top, followed by the Diaspora Jews (principally Hellenists), with proselytes and God-fearers next, and Samaritans (whom Jews regarded as heretics) and Gentiles at the bottom. Of course this order held true only for those who believed Judaism had some value. A pagan Roman soldier would not have cared a mite that he was at the bottom of the local religious system. He was on top of the international political system. But within Judaism, and in the context of Acts, this social order was very important.

Luke, the writer of Acts, was likely a Gentile from Syrian Antioch, writing to Theophilus, a fellow Greek (1:1). Thus the issue of culture and religion was bound to influence Acts because both its author and its recipient had non-Palestinian backgrounds.

## Narrow Apostles, Broad Spirit

The book opens just after the resurrection and moves quickly to Christ's last appearance to the apostles. Our Lord's final words before his ascension are recorded in Acts

1:8: "You shall receive power when the Holy Spirit has come upon you; and you shall be my witnesses in Jerusalem and in all Judea and Samaria and to the end of the earth."

As we saw in the last chapter, early in Jesus' ministry he had taken the disciples with him into Samaria (Jn. 4). He had observed, however, that they were not yet ready to deal with the Samaritans. They still considered the Samaritans second class. So when Jesus later sent the disciples out two by two, he instructed them, "Go nowhere among the Gentiles, and enter no town of the Samaritans" (Mt. 10:5). In Acts 1:8, however, he says explicitly that when the Holy Spirit has come upon them, they will then be ready to go both to the Samaritans and to the Gentiles. Jesus had already told them that it was necessary that he leave in order that the Spirit could come (Jn. 16:7). The Spirit would do through Jesus' disciples what Jesus himself could not. Jesus could not go out to all the ends of the earth, but his body, the church, can.

Today it is still the Spirit of God who does his work through us. Only as we are sensitive to where (literally) that Spirit is taking us is our work significant. Jesus wants us to be empty vessels that God can enter and use, to be present in and to be sensitive to cultures quite different from our own. This incarnational evangelism, this unique partnership through which God builds his worldwide church is the subject of Acts.

The work of the Spirit in us, however, does not obliterate our personality or eliminate our limitations. The humanity of the apostles is evident even in Peter's first sermon at Pentecost.

The disciples were together for this feast, one of the three major events of the Jewish calendar. While Jerusalem was already a multiethnic town, it was even more so at Pentecost when Jews from around the world made pilgrimage to the Holy City. Who were these people? "Parthians and

Medes and Elamites and residents of Mesopotamia, Judea and Cappadocia, Pontus and Asia, Phrygia and Pamphylia, Egypt and the parts of Libya belonging to Cyrene [way over in North Africa], and visitors from Rome, both Jews and proselytes, Cretans and Arabians" (2:9-11).

They did not only come for religious purposes, but also to find out what was going on in the rest of the world and to bring that news back. This formed a communication network, much of it centered around Jerusalem. The pilgrims usually came to Jerusalem for the Passover feast and stayed until the time of Pentecost (fifty days later).[1] This international group, temporarily in Jerusalem, was soon to return to their nations scattered around the world. But while they were in Jerusalem, they observed the crucifixion and heard the preaching of the apostles. Many of these Diaspora Jews would have carried this news of the Messiah quickly over long distances when they returned to their homes, almost immediately fulfilling the Great Commission of Acts 1:8.

Peter, however, even after being filled by the Spirit, did not have God's work so clearly in mind as the Spirit did. A crowd had gathered around the disciples. "Now there were dwelling in Jerusalem Jews, devout men from every nation under heaven. And at this sound the multitude came together, and they were bewildered, because each one heard them speaking in his own language. And they were amazed and wondered, saying, 'Are not all these who are speaking Galileans? And how is it that we hear, each of us in his own native language?' " (2:5-8).

Peter's limited viewpoint is seen in his opening statement of explanation to this crowd of people from over fifteen nations: "Men of Judea and all who dwell in Jerusalem" (2:14). He then proceeds to quote an extended passage from the Old Testament (Joel 2:28-32) to explain that the disciples are not drunk but Spirit-filled. What this multinational crowd hears in this Spirit-inspired choice of words is, "I will pour out my Spirit on all people. . . . And everyone who calls on the name of the Lord will be saved" (2:17, 21 NIV). They applied this invitation to themselves. But Peter's myopia continues: "Men of Israel, hear these words: Jesus of Nazareth . . ." (2:22). Nonetheless, the Spirit moved three thousand to respond to the message (2:41), and we can assume they included many of the nations represented in the crowd.

## A Case of De Facto Segregation

This cultural myopia continued to plague the apostles in the early days of the church. As I already mentioned, not only were there synagogues for different language groups (Aramaic, Greek and so on) and different ethnic groups (Egyptians, Mesopotamians, Cretans and so on) but even for different trades (such as copperworkers). The pattern of house churches within the early Christian community tended to preserve this cultural diversity as believers gathered to worship in already de facto segregated neighborhoods and synagogues. Since all the apostles came from synagogues of Palestinian Jews, they also unintentionally remained isolated from Christian converts who attended synagogues of Hellenistic Jews.

This situation eventually threatened to divide the growing Christian community as it had the Jewish community. The problem surfaced when "the Hellenists murmured against the Hebrews because their widows were neglected in the daily distribution" (6:1). The Hellenists were likely Christian converts from among Jews belonging to Greek-speaking synagogues. The Hebrews mentioned most probably were Christian converts from among the Aramaic-speaking Palestinian Jews, of which the apostles were twelve.

The Hellenists quite naturally began to feel isolated

*84*

from the power and communication network of the early church. When goods were being handed out to those in need in the Christian community, the Hellenists did not get the word until it was too late. But the word got out quickly among those who were close to the power structure of the apostles—Aramaic-speaking Palestinians. Even if the Hellenists did get the message, they felt the distribution was weighted unfairly and neglected their needy ones.

The communication problem was compounded, however, among those Hellenists who did not attend Temple services. Even before the time of Jesus, a radical attitude toward the Law and the Temple had developed among some of them. They felt that the letter of the Law could be laxed if its spiritual lessons were kept and that prayer could substitute for Temple sacrifices.[2] With this devalued view of what Palestinian Jews held in high esteem, the Hellenists were likely to go to the Temple far less often than the Hebrews. And as Acts 5:42 reveals, the apostles were regularly in the Temple as well as in their segregated house churches. "Every day in the temple and at home they did not cease teaching and preaching Jesus Christ."

This same sort of de facto segregation and isolation happens all the time today. A group of two dozen Korean pastors fellowship together regularly in one eastern city, but no one else knows they exist. There are also vast numbers of minority and urban churches that are blocked out of the entire evangelical communication system; for example, six or eight White evangelical presses compete to sell more and more literature to the suburban churches who can afford to buy. Meanwhile, the Black churches of America are saying, "There is no literature for our people." The question is, What is our response?

## Splitting Power with a Minority

The apostles were men of God. I am not criticizing them.

I am only saying what the Bible says. They were human beings who failed. They knew it. And when they saw their failure, they said, "Okay, Lord. What do you want us to do about it? How should we respond?"

"The twelve summoned the body of disciples and said, 'It is not right that we should give up preaching the word of God to serve tables. Therefore, brethren, pick out from among you seven men of good repute, full of the Spirit and of wisdom, whom we may appoint to this duty. But we will devote ourselves to prayer and to the ministry of the word.' And what they said pleased the whole multitude, and they chose Stephen, a man full of faith and of the Holy Spirit, and Philip, and Prochorus, and Nicanor, and Timon, and Parmenas, and Nicolaus, a proselyte of Antioch" (6:3-5).

Notice the names. Stephen and Philip are not Jewish names. Prochorus is certainly not a Jewish name, nor are Nicanor, Timon and Parmenas. Then notice this last fellow, Nicolaus, a proselyte from Antioch. Nicolaus was not even a Jew; he was a Gentile who had become a Jew through circumcision. The apostles were not simply having people chosen to distribute the goods. They recognized that the Hellenists felt isolated from the power structure of the whole community. The Aramaic-speaking converts were already well represented, so the apostles established a second power structure. They pulled out from the Hellenists a group of leaders who would be recognized by the apostles. They changed the structure. They split the power to overcome the de facto segregation.

Some may be wondering how you can reach Blacks on campus or through your church. Have you ever thought of putting two of them in your top leadership or creating a second leadership group for Blacks? You may find that other Blacks are much more willing to become involved if they have a piece of the power structure. If you simply ask them to come in at the bottom, you are implying that they must work their way up. We should imitate the apostles. They saw that right from the beginning they had to give equality of power.

They were not establishing two churches but simply delegating authority. The important fact is that they recognized cultural diversity as a valid reason for division of power. Mission societies around the world are faced by irate national churches who want the right to have power over their own affairs. Why must money given by American churches be spent only by American missionaries? The conflict lies not in their ignorance but in our unwillingness to accept a Spirit-filled national who is responsible directly to the Holy Spirit. Giving them this right and power frees the national to use national values and lines of communication. Similarly, the Black and White rift in this country will not be settled by inviting Blacks merely to join White churches, but rather by recognizing a Black power structure that is responsible directly to the Holy Spirit.

Many evangelical Blacks are saying, for example, "Why is it that we can't get any students into Christian schools?" A Christian school could respond by saying, "Okay. We'll establish a quota system. Four or five Black leaders from, let's say, the National Black Evangelical Association can select any twenty-five Black students that they want trained, send them to us and we will accept them, carte blanche, without any further selection process." Doing this would begin to train the real leaders within the Black community. Now that's radical, but it's biblical.

What was the result of the apostles' action? "The word of God increased; and the number of the disciples multiplied greatly in Jerusalem" (6:7). The men who were chosen to distribute the food because they were "of good repute, full of the Spirit" also became filled with grace and power (6:8).

Philip, one of the seven men, went on to preach in Samaria where the apostles had not gone since the resurrection. The apostles became a bit concerned and decided to send an investigative delegation (8:4-25). "Now when the apostles at Jerusalem heard that Samaria had received the word of God, they sent to them Peter and John, who came down and prayed for them that they might receive the Holy Spirit; for it had not yet fallen on any of them, but they had only been baptized in the name of the Lord Jesus. Then they laid their hands on them and they received the Holy Spirit" (8:14-17). Peter and John stayed around a while observing, recognizing their faith to be genuine. As a result, the faith of the apostles was stretched.

I suggest that the reason the Spirit of God came on the Samaritans only after the apostles laid hands on them was more for Peter and John, who were not quite sure that the Samaritans were fit for inclusion in the church, than for the Samaritans. Only when they saw the Spirit of God active in people outside their own tight Judean context did they believe that extending the gospel to those who were not strictly Jews was proper. They returned to Jerusalem and broadened the vision of the believers there by including the Samaritans, a socially outcast people, among the faithful. They recognized them, without distinction, as full-fledged members of God's family. This view is confirmed in that Jerusalem never sent another delegation or imposed their leadership on the Samaritans. Rather they were allowed to continue to grow and develop as an indigenous movement without outside intervention.

But the understanding of those in Jerusalem was still inadequate. While the apostles were preaching in the Temple every morning, Philip met an Ethiopian (probably a Black) and told him that he too could believe. Presumably the man returned to his own land to preach the gospel there (8:26-39).

Stephen, another one of the seven, "did great wonders

and signs among the people" (6:8), and then he went to the "synagogue of the Freedmen (as it was called)" (6:9).[3] This is the first time Acts mentions that somebody went with the gospel to the Diaspora community in Jerusalem. Notice it was a man who came out of this community. Apparently the apostles had never been there. As soon as he was given authority, Stephen began to use it to communicate the gospel.

Suddenly, in the act of sharing power and authority with a minority, the church burst its cultural bonds and reached not only that minority, the Hellenists, but also the Samaritans and the Ethiopians. The full implications of this had not fully dawned on the apostles, but God was doing a work, the completion of which will be seen in the next chapter.

Although Philip received an open response to his message, the reaction Stephen received in the synagogue of the Freedmen was quite different.

**Stephen the Hellenist**
The synagogue Stephen addressed included people from Cyrene (in North Africa), Alexandria (in Egypt), Cilicia and Asia (in what is now Turkey). They were either proselytes or they were brought up in Jewish homes in these different countries. They were Jewish, but they were considered second-class Jews who were struggling to become part of the first class.

From their midst arose a reaction to Stephen far more heated than even the Pharisees' response to the apostles. Some of his opponents interpreted his teaching as an attack on the Law and the Temple. But he preached with such wisdom that none of them could stand up to him. They were so enraged that they trumped up charges against him and brought him before the Sanhedrin. This at first may seem surprising, since I have already indicated that some Hellenistic Jews had their own radical views of the Law and the Temple. Understanding this tension among Hellenistic Jews themselves begins with a basic understanding of the nature of ethnicity.

The most red-white-and-blue Americans are often second-generation people out of an ethnic community. Those with strong ethnic identity have a name for them. If they are Chinese, they call them bananas (yellow outside, white inside). If they are Indians, they call them apples (red outside, white inside). If they are Black, they call them Oreos or Uncle Toms. Those who are trying to move out of a second-class ethnic community and become part of a first-class melting-pot community are the most defensive of the rights and sanctity of the first-class community. They are also the quickest to dismiss and reject unique aspects of their background that reveal their second-class ethnicity.

Of course if you ask these second-generation peoples about the others, they'll say, "Oh, they are just radicals trying to take us down the road of nonexistence. We're trying to build peace in society." So there are two points of view which frequently show up as culture develops and changes. The nature of culture is to define in-groups and out-groups because that's how culture gives us security. We have a way to tell who is safe and who is not.

This tension among those who were changing over to the dominant culture may well have been a principal cause of the reaction to Stephen's message. While Diaspora Jews tended to devalue the Temple, some were even more attached to it than even the Pharisees and rabbinate. They also tended to accept less from their surrounding culture than other Hellenists.[4] Stephen had come into this synagogue preaching something that was not pure Judaism. These Hellenists got angry and accused him. They wanted to please, to make points with the Palestinians. They were not concerned with being Egyptian. They were giving up their Egyptianness in order to try to become more Palestinian. So when they brought Stephen to the Sanhedrin they were saying in effect, 'We want to show you how much we identify with you. Here is a bad man; we're accusing him before you. Listen to him, and then you'll see how good we are and how committed to you we are." They were so intense in this that they even "set up false witnesses who said, 'This man never ceases to speak words against this holy place and the law'" (6:13).

Stephen now stands before the high priest. He has been brought by the Freedmen out of the synagogue to defend himself in the Temple courtroom against the charges of condemning the Temple and the Law. On one side sits the high priest and the Sanhedrin. On the other is a motley group of Hellenistic Jews, from all over the world, who are angry because Stephen is not speaking the truth as they see it. They have brought him in before the Jewish establishment. Stephen is given an opportunity to defend himself. That is a tight spot for a Hellenist to be in.

In 1970 Tom Skinner was asked to come to the Urbana Student Missions Convention and talk about what Black Christians are thinking. A lot of White people heard for the first time what Black Christians have been saying for a long, long time. It shocked them. Many people were unhappy with Andrew Young as our ambassador to the U.N. But when Young, for example, said that there were political prisoners in the United States, he was saying nothing more than what people in the Black community have been saying for many years. In fact, he was extremely conservative in the way he spoke. But when it came through to the White community, it sounded radical. Andrew Young may not have been able to understand why people were getting so confused and upset. After all, he was only saying what he had always heard, and what he knows to be true.

Stephen does the same when he stands up before the

Sanhedrin: he begins to say some of the things that he has heard ever since he was a boy. "Brethren and fathers, hear me. The God of glory appeared to our father Abraham, when he was in Mesopotamia" (7:2). Immediately Stephen is on the offensive. Abraham was not from Palestine. In fact God's glory first appeared to him outside this land, considered so important. "And [God] said to him, 'Depart from your land and from your kindred and go into the land which I will show you.' Then he departed from the land of the Chaldeans and lived in Haran [near Asia Minor]" (7:3-4). Even after receiving the promise Abraham did not go straight to Palestine. He was in no rush to get to the so-called sacred land. Maybe his father had greater priority at that time. "And after his father died, God removed him from there into this land [Israel] in which you are now living; yet he gave him no inheritance in it, not even a foot's length, but promised to give it to him in possession and to his posterity after him, though he had no child. And God spoke to this effect, that his posterity would be aliens in a land belonging to others [Egypt], who would enslave them and ill-treat them four hundred years. . . . And he gave him the covenant of circumcision. And so Abraham became the father of Isaac, and circumcised him on the eighth day; and Isaac became the father of Jacob, and Jacob of the twelve patriarchs" (7:4-8).

Abraham, the founding father of Judaism, never got one foot of his land. It was promised only to his children. So much for the Palestinian claims on Abraham, argues Stephen. Not only that, but it was after God appeared to Abraham, after the promise was given and after God began moving Abraham, that the sign of circumcision was given. The issues for Gentiles seeking to become Jews was, "Will you be circumcised or not?" This was a fixture of Jewishness that Stephen claims is only important in the context of an ongoing relationship with God—quite a contrast to the Palestinian position.[5]

Stephen continues. "And the patriarchs, jealous of Joseph, sold him into Egypt; but God was with him, and rescued him out of all his afflictions, and gave him favor and wisdom before Pharaoh, king of Egypt who made him governor over Egypt and over all his household" (7:9-10). Stephen is drawing a comparison between Abraham who never got a piece of his land and Joseph who was booted out of the land by his brothers, the patriarchs. While this bunch of rumscullions sent him down into Egypt, it was the Egyptians who gave him proper honor. Joseph was identifying with Egyptian culture. He was absorbing their wisdom while helping them to survive as a nation by overcoming the seven-year famine.

Remember some of the people in the synagogue are Egyptians. Stephen reminds them that Abraham was a Mesopotamian and that it was the Egyptians, not the patriarchs who lived in Palestine, who took good care of Joseph. Imagine how this is beginning to set with the Pharisees!

Stephen keeps on building his case. "And Joseph sent and called to him Jacob his father and all his kindred, seventy-five souls; and Jacob went down into Egypt. And he died, himself and our fathers, and they were carried back to Shechem [in Israel]" (7:14-16). In other words, the early home of the nation, the place where even the patriarchs died, was Egypt. They too became Egyptian. And that, Stephen was implying, is who many of us Hellenists are. We are full Jews, nonetheless.

After four hundred years of Egyptian rule,

Moses was born, and was beautiful before God. And he was brought up for three months in his father's house; and when he was exposed, Pharaoh's daughter adopted him and brought him up as her own son. And Moses was instructed in all the wisdom of the Egyptians, and he was

*93*

mighty in his words and deeds. When he was forty years old, it came into his heart to visit his brethren, the sons of Israel. And seeing one of them being wronged, he defended the oppressed man and avenged him by striking the Egyptian. He supposed that his brethren understood that God was giving them deliverance by his hand, but they did not understand. And on the following day he appeared to them as they were quarreling and would have reconciled them, saying, "Men, you are brethren, why do you wrong each other?" But the man who was wronging his neighbor thrust him aside, saying, "Who made you a ruler and judge over us? Do you want to kill me as you killed the Egyptian yesterday?" At this retort Moses fled, and became an exile in the land of Midian. (7:20-29)

Not only had the nation been influenced by being in Egypt four hundred years, but Moses, the greatest leader and prophet of the Jews, was so Egyptian that his contemporary Jews (the fathers of Stephen's listeners) rejected him (as is seen in 6:36). Even when Moses fled, did he go to the Promised Land of Palestine? Not even then. He went to Midian. That did not set well with the Pharisees either.

Stephen has more. "Now when forty years had passed, an angel appeared to him in the wilderness of Mount Sinai" (7:30). Where is God? He is out in the wilderness. And God says to Moses, " 'I am the God of your fathers, the God of Abraham and of Isaac and of Jacob.' And Moses trembled and did not dare to look. And the Lord said to him, 'Take off the shoes from your feet, for the place where you are standing is holy ground' " (7:32-33). Stephen has made it clear that this holy ground is not Palestine. Stephen is still not making any friends in the Sanhedrin.

Courageously he proceeds with his Hellenistic interpretation of Israel's history. "This Moses whom they refused, saying, 'Who made you a ruler and a judge?' God sent as both ruler and deliverer by the hand of the angel that appeared to him in the bush. He led them out" (7:35-36). Moses was an Egyptian-styled leader, rejected by his brothers because of this, who God ordained as just such a leader. The irony is clear to Stephen's audience.

"This is the Moses who said to the Israelites, 'God will raise up for you a prophet from your brethren as he raised me up.' " Stephen means Jesus. "This is he who was in the congregation in the wilderness with the angel who spoke to him at Mount Sinai, and with our fathers; and he received living oracles to give to us" (7:37-38). What were those "living oracles"? They were the Law, given by God to this Egyptian leader, Moses, in the Sinai wilderness—far from the "holy land."

Not until Stephen has firmly established that the patriarchs and Moses were a universal and international group does Stephen identify with his listeners: *"Our* fathers refused to obey him, but thrust him aside, and in their hearts they turned to Egypt" (7:39). In fact, they made a god like they had seen in Egypt. They were more Egyptian than they were Jewish. These were our fathers, Stephen insists.

Stephen concludes his defense on the first accusation against him: he had condemned the Law. He has taken forty-two verses to explain that the earliest part of Jewish history starts in Mesopotamia, continues in Egypt and ends in the wilderness. And the Law came in the wilderness. The Jewish nation was made up of people who came from Mesopotemia and who were more Egyptian in their hearts than anything else. He is not against the Law, just concerned with where it came from and who it came to. Stephen then defends himself against the second charge: he had condemned the Temple.

"Our fathers had the tent of witness in the wilderness, even as he who spoke to Moses directed him to make it" (7:44). In other words, not only does the Law originate in the wilderness outside the holy land, but the first tabernacle —God's dwelling place—was also in the wilderness.

Stephen then dismisses the long period of the judges (from Joshua to the monarchy) in two sentences: "Our fathers in turn brought it in with Joshua when they dispossessed the nations which God thrust out before our fathers. So it was until the days of David" (7:45). The Palestinian Jews, in contrast, would have picked up their history at the Jordan River with Joshua because this was the beginning of the history of Israel's relationship to the land. They gave scant attention to what happened before that. They were concerned with the holy land as the place where God dwelt, for it gave them a position of privilege.

Stephen sweeps by that whole section of history in one short sentence and deals with the Temple. "David ... found favor in the sight of God and asked leave to find a habitation for the God of Jacob. But it was Solomon who built a house for him. Yet the Most High does not dwell in houses made with hands; as the prophet says, 'Heaven is my throne, and earth my footstool. What house will you build for me, says the Lord, or what is the place of my rest? Did not my hand make all these things?' " (7:45-50). So much for the Temple, rooted as it is to one particular locality and controlled by a privileged fragment of God's people. It cannot possibly contain God.

**A Religious Lynch Mob**

By this time the members of the Sanhedrin were very agitated. The Hellenists who had charged Stephen saw that they were losing the argument, and became nervous and angry. They saw that they had brought in somebody who made the Palestinian Jews look foolish. Stephen, seeing that he had little time left, thrusts to the heart the sword of truth: "You stiff-necked people, uncircumcised in heart and ears, you always resist the Holy Spirit. As your fathers did, so do you. Which of the prophets did not your fathers persecute? And they killed those who announced beforehand the coming of the Righteous One, whom you have now betrayed and murdered, you who have received the law as delivered by angels and did not keep it" (7:51-53). That was as far as he got. "When they heard these things they were enraged, and they ground their teeth against him. But he, full of the Holy Spirit, gazed into heaven and saw the glory of God, and Jesus standing at the right hand of God" (7:54-55).

This same group of men had heard John and Peter defend the faith. And they had been a little upset about these Galilean Jews who to their minds were a little bit wrong. They punished them mildly and put them in jail for a while. But they had not been very upset because, as Gamaliel pointed out, every twenty years someone comes along claiming to be the Messiah and gathering a following. But it never amounts to much. "Let them alone; for if this plan . . . is of men, it will fail; but if it is of God, you will not be able to overthrow them" (5:38-39).

Stephen's message, however, so infuriated them that they immediately took him out to stone him to death (7:56-60). Stephen's explosive message made Judaism a universal faith. Anyone could come to God and be fully related to him without adopting an ethnocentric, Palestinian form of the religion. The Palestinian position of privilege, according to Stephen, was a sham.

I once thought of Stephen as a pious little angel who stood quietly while they stoned him. But now I see a man of faith, a man of prayer, a radical not because he wanted to be, but because he had been driven up against the wall. He would not run; he was standing for truth. He was saying, "I'm in the hands of God. I've said my piece and now God can do with it what he wants."

Christians have got to stand for truth. We have got to

realize that being meek does not mean being weak. This does not mean being aggressive either, but simply being willing to be steadfast for the truth, the truth of a universal gospel that is not bound by culture. That is what Stephen did.

# 7
# Unified but Not Uniform: Acts (Part Two)

PAUL, OR SAUL AS LUKE IDENTIFIES him in Acts 7—9, now enters the developing story of the early church. He had heard Stephen's powerful defense of God's world-embracing promise and plan, but went with the mob, out of the city, to the place of stoning. And how did he react to what he had heard and seen? With absolute rage.

He watched the coats of those who laid them aside to get better throws at Stephen and consented to his death (7:58, 8:1). He ravaged the church, "entering house after house, he dragged off men and women and committed them to prison" (8:3). Some time later he was "still breathing threats and murder against the disciples of the Lord" (9:1). Stephen's message had a profound impact on this bright, young Pharisee. Luke's mention of Paul's presence at the trial and stoning indicates it to be an important turning point.

Though Stephen's basic message was the same as that of

Peter and John (who had already been tried by the Sanhedrin and dismissed as not overly dangerous), Paul could
see that Stephen carried the implications of this new message far beyond the provincial boundaries and concerns
of Palestinian Judaism. This threatened the whole structure of Judaism as Paul and his fellow Pharisees understood
it. This was something the message of John and Peter did
not (yet) do. This kind of message had to be destroyed.

When the Holy Spirit begins to convict someone the first
response can be absolute anger—screaming, ranting and
raving before final submission. That's what happened to
Paul. He ranted and raved and persecuted the early church
until Jesus finally got hold of him. But when Paul was con-
verted, he says in Galatians, he did not go back to Jerusalem
to learn from Peter and the other apostles (Gal. 1:16-18).
Instead he went out to the wilderness (presumably to re-
study the Old Testament). He was already a scholar of the
Scriptures, but he had heard Stephen dig some stuff out
that he never knew was there. He went back through the
Scriptures with a question in his mind. What does this teach
me of Jesus Christ? He began to uncover all kinds of things.
The letter to the Galatians provides one important summary of his findings. He says the gospel in its entirety was
given to Abraham. The Law which was given four hundred
years later was only the schoolmaster to bring us to Jesus
Christ. But the message given to Abraham (before the Law,
before circumcision) applies to anyone from any nation
who has the same faith as Abraham. That is why he called
himself an apostle to the Gentiles. Paul had been freed. His
outline of the gospel in Galatians is almost the same outline
that Stephen gave.

After Paul's third missionary journey he was arrested
in the Temple by Hellenists, as Stephen had been (21:27).
They accused him of the same crime of speaking against the
Law and the Temple (21:28). Paul evidently associated

these events with Stephen's death for when he addresses the people from the stairway, he dwells on his own persecution of the early church which arose out of Stephen's defense (22:4). Then he refers specifically to his witness and approval of Stephen's death (22:20). His next statement is that he received the commission from God to go to the Gentiles (22:21). Paul was arrested by the same kind of people, in the same city, for the same crime as Stephen, and in his message he associated Stephen with his call to the Gentiles. So even eighteen years later, Paul identified with Stephen greatly.

**To the Gentiles Also**
The apostle's provincialism, noted earlier, continued to the time recorded in Acts 8 where the church in Jerusalem could hardly believe what had happened in Samaria. The difficulty in overcoming their narrowness with non-Palestinian Jews could only be intensified with people who weren't any kind of Jews. Were even *they* candidates for God's saving message?

The opening of the fellowship of the children of God to uncircumcised, untaught, heathen (Gentiles) was a completely new concept for which there had been no precedent. The spreading of the gospel had moved from the purest Palestinian Jews to the Greek-influenced Hellenists to the Samaritans and the Ethiopian eunuch—all with the Holy Spirit's strong influence. Yet each of these come out of a Hebrew tradition. The ultimate test of the universality of the gospel was for a Palestinian Jew to go to a Gentile. Circumcision was the symbol that one accepted faith in God as expressed in Abraham. It also symbolized that you agreed to follow the Law of a specific culture expressed in a particular language.

In the minds of every Jew, coming to God was a cultural process, a civilizing process manifest in a change of behavior. To accept God without learning that behavior was not possible because God had communicated himself through the behavior prescribed in the Old Testament. They had no way of conceptualizing how a heathen could believe in God through any other means—including Jesus Christ.

In Acts 10 God acts dramatically to correct this misunderstanding. The story of the meeting between Cornelius the Roman centurion and Peter the apostle begins on a rooftop in a Judean seaport called Joppa. Resting before lunch, Peter receives a vision of ritually unclean food being presented to him and a voice that says, "Eat!" Three times the vision occurs and three times Peter argues with the Spirit (10:9-16). It is encouraging for me to see the fear and disbelief Peter expresses as he realizes in a dream what God is asking him to do. Peter is no superhuman missionary on a pedestal; he is the same weak Peter who followed Jesus. Today, like then, the gospel will not naturally cross cultural boundaries, but only with great sensitivity to the leading of the Spirit can we build bridges of communication.

The Spirit demonstrates the importance of Peter's vision by simultaneously giving Cornelius a vision thirty-five miles north in the town of Caesarea. The Spirit instructs Cornelius to send for Peter (10:1-8). The Spirit instructs Peter to go with the messengers (10:19-20). No other incident in Acts shows the Spirit so explicitly involving himself in human actions. Every detail is set down; there is no room for uncertainties.

The Spirit uses the natural bridge of selecting a Gentile who is favorable to the Jewish community, familiar with the Hebrew faith, and who worships God. Yet Cornelius has not been circumcised. Further, he has invited his relatives as well as friends to be with him (10:24). It is quite clear to Peter that if this group joins the church there will be no end to where this thing can go! When they meet, Peter tells

Cornelius of his own perplexity. Yet he acts on what the Spirit told him to do (10:28-29).

The story is a clear case of a man who is beyond his understanding of cultural possibility, acting on knowledge that has been given to him from another source—God's revealed truth.

Cornelius explains that he wants to hear God's Word from Peter, who willingly obliges. The house full of Gentiles believes his message and the Holy Spirit comes down on them all. Peter and the witnesses who came with him cannot deny that this is of the Holy Spirit (10:30-48).

Culture, I mentioned before, defines for us what is possible and what is not. What is not possible for you may be possible for someone in other cultural contexts. It is impossible for us to communicate with trees or rocks. But those in animistic cultures do it daily, or at least they believe they do. Christ blew down the cultural possibility-impossibility barriers and let Peter see that we have to live in the realms of the "impossible." The church today is not used to believing the impossible. Therefore when we see it written out in black and white, we reject it. We have been enclosed by cultural walls that are knocked flat when we see God at work in our lives.

Peter now had to explain this seeming impossibility to the people back home. "Now the apostles and the brethren who were in Judea heard that the Gentiles also had received the word of God. So when Peter went up to Jerusalem, the circumcision party criticized him, saying, 'Why did you go to uncircumcised men and eat with them?' " (11:1-3). The "apostles and the brethren who were in Judea" or certainly the "circumcision party," though Christians, still did not understand that Jesus had come to be far more than a Jewish Messiah; they still did not understand that he had come to reconcile everyone to God and to each other, breaking down all dividing walls such as the one dividing Jews and

*103*

Gentiles. "But Peter began and explained to them in order" (11:4).

Luke considers this episode so important that he repeats the whole story of Peter and Cornelius through Peter's report in Acts 11:5-17. He does so because the conclusion to which this experience leads them and which is the culmination of much of what Luke records in the first eleven chapters of Acts is one of the most significant verses in the New Testament. "When they heard this [Peter's report] they were silenced. And they glorified God, saying, *'Then to the Gentiles also God has granted repentance unto life'* " (11:18).

What a giant step this is for this group of intensely religious, intensely nationalistic Jews who had followed Jesus for three years without ever quite seeing what he really was trying to do. Suddenly they are awakened to the fact that the gospel of Jesus Christ is for the whole world. For if a raw, heathen, uncircumcised Gentile may, without any purification process, be brought directly into the church, then certainly the gospel excludes no one.

Hundreds of years of hard-nosed prejudice was transformed—in an instant. The prejudice between Jews and Gentiles was as sharp and bitter as any we experience in the world today—Black-White, Jew-Arab, rich-poor, communist-capitalist. We know that this was not the end of the struggle within the church, but these early Christians responded to the Spirit's intervention by beginning to rid themselves of prejudice and all invidious distinctions based on notions of privilege and superiority.

**Barnabas: The Bicultural Reconciler**
Acts 11:18-20 is the cultural hinge of the book. Acts 11:18 marks the end of Luke's account of how the mind of the church grew to match God's plan. Acts 11:19-20 marks the beginning of how the church actively began to live out what they had learned and so become a truly multicultural

church. This new part begins by referring to Stephen's death and the persecution that followed (see 8:1) which resulted in a geographic expansion of the people of God. These same verses, however, also indicate that the cultural issue was still to be worked out practically.

"Now those who were scattered because of the persecution that arose over Stephen traveled as far as Phoenicia and Cyprus and Antioch, speaking the word to none except Jews" (11:19). The Hellenistic Jewish Christians from Jerusalem went into Greek areas but only spoke to other Hellenistic Jews about Jesus. This was a perfectly normal process—people seek out their own kind in new areas.

When the Chinese come from Taiwan into San Francisco or New York, they seek out the Chinese community. If they are Christians, they find the Chinese church and identify with that. Some of them have been in such communities in this country for three generations and have never belonged to any other church. When the Blacks from Atlanta go to New York, they find certain churches that appeal to Blacks from Atlanta which are different from the churches that appeal to Blacks from Alabama. When you go into a Black church in New York City, it does not take long to find out where its roots go back, because they all have their roots either in the South, in the West Indies or somewhere in Africa. It is important to understand this in talking with such people. Our cities are filled with Korean, Chinese, Spanish, Black and White churches that have lines of communication that go back to a homeland.

When I went to Africa, I found the same tendency in myself. It was very easy for me to stay in the mission station and fellowship with the other American missionaries there. That is where I was comfortable. I had to force myself to get out of the mission station and down into the village to deal with people who spoke an unfamiliar language, ate unfamiliar food, held unfamiliar values and functioned in an unfamiliar culture. It was difficult to communicate the gospel in that setting. It took deliberate discipline to do that because naturally, of myself, I would have stayed on the mission station. I think this is precisely what many of these Hellenistic Jewish converts did. They went to the Jewish communities; they found their own kind of people; they felt comfortable there; and they began to share the gospel. That was wonderful, but it was not reaching the uttermost parts of the earth.

But not all these scattered Hellenists spoke only to Jews. "There were some of them, men of Cyprus and Cyrene, who on coming to Antioch spoke to the Greeks also, preaching the Lord Jesus" (11:20). So in the city of Antioch, some evangelized Jews only and some began to evangelize Gentiles as well. If Hellenistic Jewish Christians and Palestinian Jewish Christians had their problems (as we saw in Acts 6), what will happen when Gentiles start believing in Jesus? "The hand of the Lord was with them, and a great number that believed turned to the Lord. News of this came to the ears of the church in Jerusalem" (11:21-22). What news? News that for the first time large numbers of Gentiles were becoming Christians. Note that this comes in the context of the story of Cornelius and the truth that Jesus is Lord of all, that there is to be no division in the body of Christ. How would the potential conflict in Antioch between the two groups be dealt with? Jerusalem decided to send somebody. "They sent Barnabas to Antioch" (11:22). Why did they send him? "Joseph . . . was surnamed by the apostles Barnabas (which means, Son of encouragement), a Levite, a native of Cyprus" (4:36). He was a reconciler; he brought people together. He consoled in the biblical sense of the word. He was also a Levite who spoke Hebrew, living in Jerusalem but born in Cyprus, who thus understood Greek and the Hellenistic peoples. He was a bicultural man whose gift was consolation, pulling people together. Now in Antioch there were Jewish and Gentile believers, some of them from Cyprus, and they needed to learn how to live together. Barnabas was the man to do the job.

Later, when Barnabas decided he needed help, he did not go back to Cyprus. He did not go back to Jerusalem. He went north to Tarsus to find another bicultural man—Paul, a Roman citizen who was also a Pharisee. Barnabas knew Paul's conversion as well as his background. He introduced Paul to the apostles shortly after his conversion. He had seen the effect on Paul of Stephen's message of a universal God as Paul argued with Hellenists in Jerusalem. The opposition this created caused Paul to retreat to his Hellenistic home town of Tarsus where he no doubt also had a bicultural ministry (9:26-30).

A common misconception is that Paul received his name when he became a Christian. Rather, he used his original Jewish name, Saul, primarily when in a Jewish setting. Of course, once he began dealing more with Gentiles, he used his Roman name, Paul. The two names are therefore another reflection of how well suited he was for this special role at Antioch.

An important principle emerges from this episode. When there is potential for division, do not focus on it. Find someone who is able to be a consoler, who can bring people together. "When he [Barnabas] came and saw the grace of God, he was glad; and he exhorted them all to remain faithful to the Lord with steadfast purpose" (11:23). The centrality of Christ is the message for such a consoler. That is the only ground on which we can hope to build one church. If he had focused on which language they should use or on circumcision, they would have split down the middle. Instead Barnabas preached Jesus Christ to both groups. He said, "Focus on Jesus Christ. That is where your unity lies. Come to understand *him*. You Jews, you've got to realize that these Greeks have a little different understanding of who Jesus is."

How do we know he succeeded in keeping them together? Because it says, "In Antioch the disciples were for the first time called Christians" (11:26). If you have peaches and pears, and put them in the same bowl, you have to come up with a new word to describe them. If you have Jews and Gentiles and put them in the same place, you have to come up with a new word too. You have a phenomenon that has to have an identity. The name probably came from outsiders, but it highlights the believers' focus on Jesus Christ. When they considered what was their common ground, they could not find it anywhere except in the fact that they both cleaved to Jesus. This is a powerful message to our campuses and churches if we can see Blacks, Chinese, Hispanics, Whites, northerners, southerners—whatever diversity we have—hang together on the name of the Lord Jesus Christ. They became one in Christ first in Antioch.

The last paragraph of Acts 11 cites the material aid the church of Antioch sends to the church of Jerusalem (11:27-30). This suggests first that the church in Antioch was able to unite on practical matters, that their oneness was not in name only. Second, it suggests a mature, coequal relationship between the two churches. Acts 12 continues this theme of the declining role of Jerusalem and the growing status of Antioch.

The death of James must have been a shocking experience to those in Jerusalem (12:1-2). Peter's arrest is turned around by an angelic visit (12:3-17), but the picture of a fearful group of disciples behind locked doors who prayed for Peter's release is a stark contrast to the early chapters of Acts. The final section gives some relief in the death of Herod (12:18-24). Nonetheless, the chapter ends with Paul, Barnabas and their fresh recruit, John Mark, heading back to Antioch (12:25).

## Antioch: The Multicultural, Missionary-minded Church

Chapter 13 opens by illustrating the same principle we saw in Acts 6—splitting power multiplies the ministry. "Now in the church at Antioch there were prophets and teachers, Barnabas, Simeon who was called Niger, Lucius of Cyrene, Manaen a member of the court of Herod the tetrarch, and Saul. While they were worshiping the Lord and fasting, the Holy Spirit said, 'Set apart for me Barnabas and Saul for the work to which I have called them.' Then after fasting and praying they laid their hands on them and sent them off" (13:1-3). Note that each of the leaders (the prophets and teachers) is identified by his ethnic background (except for Barnabas and Paul who we already know about). Notice also that Barnabas and Paul are not listed together. They are not at the top of the heap, lording it over the other three. They are not at the bottom, as if to say in false humility that they do not have any influence. They are coequal leaders, and so Luke splits them, I think, purposely to show this. Again we see that the unity of the church in Antioch is more than superficial. Each leader probably represented an ethnic contingent. Simeon was Black. Lucius was Greek. Manaen was Jewish. An African. An Asian. A Palestinian.

These not only represented different ethnic and geographical areas, but almost certainly different language groups. Since people usually desire to pray in the language of their homeland, it is almost certain that Antioch followed the pattern of house churches started in Jerusalem. These house churches, however, would represent different languages as well—Aramaic likely in the Jewish sector and Greek (the trade language) for most of the others. It is probable that these three elders in Antioch were elected to represent smaller groups of believers.

This group were not leaders in name only. They had power to act on behalf of the church in setting aside two-fifths of their leadership, the entire outside representation, to go out. This once again demonstrates a considerable degree of unity and trust within the church in Antioch.

What would a powerful church in Atlanta look like? Bring together the leaders from the Black and White communities to pray and act together regularly on behalf of the church of Atlanta, and you would see eyes being opened —much more so than one church developing a powerful ministry.

Commissioning Barnabas and Paul also indicates the kind of leadership these two were building in Antioch— strong, indigenous leadership. It was like saying, "You two have done your job. We're on our feet now. You don't have to stay. In fact, you should be out doing the same in places that need you more."

This multicultural church thus became the first missionary church. Peter preached to a mixed group at Pentecost by an accident of God. Disciples left Jerusalem after Stephen's death because of persecution. But people left Antioch because of a deliberate decision to send.

**The Jerusalem Council**
On Paul's first missionary journey, described in Acts 13— 14, we see his pattern of going to the synagogue and preaching a message that appeals to both Jew and Gentile. Within these Hellenistic communities the core leadership of devout, establishment Jews, whose authority depended on their claim to *the* truth, tended to reject Paul because he introduced new ideas. Other fringe Jews who came to the synagogue for social reasons found him irrelevant. So Paul's greatest response was from those devout Jews who genuinely wanted to know God and from Gentile Godfearers. The God-fearers would likely be skeptical at first that they could be fully accepted by God without circumcision. But their excitement would grow as later they would

tell more and more of their friends the implications of this incredible message.

When Paul arrives back in Antioch and reports to the people, his focus is on the way God opened a way for the Gentiles to believe (14:26-27). This was exciting news in Antioch! It confirmed to the people that the nature of *their* church as a multicultural community was in God's will. They rejoiced that there were many other churches like theirs. The churches of Phoenicia and Samaria, where Paul gave the same report en route to Jerusalem (15:3) had the same reaction. This contrasts sharply with the circumcision party in the Jerusalem church who wanted the Gentiles circumcised. They were adamant. Paul and Barnabas argued fiercely with them but could not resolve the situation (15:1-2).

Although the church in Jerusalem accepted in principle that Gentiles were welcome (11:18), this did not guarantee that all the people would implement that principle. The token integration of Cornelius did not guarantee that every local fellowship would welcome Gentiles. The parties thus agreed to submit their dispute to the apostles and elders in Jerusalem (15:2).

The council at Jerusalem described in Acts 15 thus deals with two important issues lying just under the surface issue of circumcision. One is the right of every church to be independently responsible to God. The second is the responsibility of churches to relate to one another. These basic issues are still with us today. The first is broken when materially wealthy churches impose their will on less-developed ones. The second principle is broken when, for example, the Black American church stops communicating with the non-Black churches because of the real, previous rejection it has experienced, or when White American churches exclude people of other backgrounds because they do not think anyone can teach them anything. "We have the teaching that others need. What could we possibly learn from African churches?"

The council of Jerusalem soon becomes an extended debate between Paul and Barnabas on the one hand and some of the Pharisees in the church on the other. Peter again recounts the story of Cornelius, pointing out that the issue of circumcision has already been resolved by the Holy Spirit (15:10-11). Finally, everyone agrees to let Paul and Barnabas speak without interruption about what actually has happened (15:12). The apostles recognize the question is not really one of circumcision, but of how Jewish Christians will relate to Gentile Christians. James's conclusion is that as far back as Amos God declared that *he* would restore his kingdom so that the Gentiles could come to him (15:16-18). The church of Antioch therefore has a right to decide its own affairs without consulting Jerusalem. "Therefore my judgment is that we should not trouble those of the Gentiles who turn to God" (15:19).

Circumcision is neither right nor wrong. But it is certainly not an essential part of the gospel.

On the other hand, James suggests that two thousand years of living under the law taught the Hebrews some important principles of God that should be passed on. If someone wants to reinvent the wheel, they are free to do so. However, it would be foolish. If the Gentiles want to painfully discover God's patterns for life, they also could do so. But it is unnecessary. James summarizes these principles as follows: the Gentiles should "abstain from the pollutions of idols and from unchastity and from what is strangled and from blood. For from early generations Moses has had in every city those who preach him, for he is read every sabbath in the synagogues" (15:20-21). These basics deal with God's impatience with putting anything before him. James's concern is to preserve the family and the health of his people.

James's first statement, better translated by NIV as "abstain from food polluted by idols," sums up years of the Hebrews' seeking after other gods while trying to remain faithful to God. A great deal of the Old Testament account leads us to the conclusion that one cannot worship God and maintain other spiritual interests. The Gentile weakness at that point would come to a head over whether or not meat offered to idols could be eaten without showing respect to the idol. It is better, says James, to stay away from anything that even looks like a compromise.[1]

The second statement of James, "abstain from ... unchastity," sums up the entire Old Testament teaching on the respect of people as people. It preserves the Old Testament teaching of the family which leads to both a healthy start for marriage (by avoiding fornication) and a healthy maintenance of a trust relationship in marriage (by avoiding adultery). Keeping sexual communication within marriage not only assures a stronger base for building the family but also prepares the larger base of love relationships on which the church itself is built. The close, personal and affectionate relationship between those who are married and the spouses of others, between married people and single people, and between singles is only possible when sexual fidelity is assured.

The third statement James makes regards the eating of strangled animals or blood. Even today we understand the importance of not eating raw meat. Modern technology and science has helped us to define more accurately the thin line between rare meat and raw meat. But in an ancient culture the best way to be sure meat has been cooked well enough to avoid disease is not to eat any meat with blood in it. Today we know that the blood spoils quicker than the meat. Every modern butcher slits the animal's throat with its hind legs suspended in the air immediately after it has been killed to allow the blood to drain out before it coagulates. Modern science has taught us the reason for this. In the Old Testament Levitical law God had not explained why but gave a long series of commandments regarding food preparation, and the nature of clean and unclean food. These laws were misused by the Pharisees and others. However, the Hebrews saw that the nations who were not as careful in their eating habits lacked the robust health of the Hebrews and often had shorter lives. The statements of James established the freedom of Antioch to do as they pleased but gave them some strong advice regarding their behavior.

Today we also should spend less time passing on our doctrinal and cultural idiosyncrasies and give more careful thought to what basic principles can be distilled from the history of Christianity in our own culture. That could be beneficial to the church's vitality in other parts of the world, or within other communities in our society.

**Both Prophet and Priest**
Some have laid much weight on the apparent rift between the Palestinian church at Jerusalem and the missionary church at Antioch, and on the apparent conflict of Peter's more provincial gospel and Paul's more Gentile gospel. I feel we must see the church of Jerusalem and the church of Antioch as manifestations of a basic tension that is essential to God's revelation of himself.

This is represented in the Old Testament by the "prophetic" and "priestly" roles. The prophets explained that God's purposes included the Gentiles and therefore demanded responsible witness to the nations. On the other hand, the priests called people in to be faithful to Jerusalem and the Temple.[2]

This split is reflected in the differing stands taken toward outsiders by the northern kingdom of Israel and the southern kingdom of Judah. Israel was involved with all the nations, and her sin was to deny the message by turning to Baal. Judah was more faithful to the message, but held Jerusalem in such high esteem that she disdained and avoided the other nations. The people in Judah could not believe that God would be angry because of such obvious faithfulness.

This dynamic is with us today in the Roman Catholic and Protestant churches. The Catholic church has tended to fulfill the priestly role by calling people into itself while the Protestant church has tended to be prophetic by sending people out into the world. Yet the two roles are seen even within Protestantism. There are evangelicals who preserve the message and liberals who seek to change social structures.

The biblical message is that the people of God can err on both sides, either by becoming so involved with action that they lose the message, or by becoming so concerned with the message that they fail to act. Faith without works is dead. Thus the church is only dynamic and powerful when both its priestly and prophetic gears are engaged.

It was in this way that the sensitive yet controlling hand of the Jerusalem church and the action-oriented hand of the Antioch church were essential to the vitality of the first-century church as a whole. Paul understood this. His missionary journey showed his compulsion to move on. Yet after each journey he insisted on returning to Jerusalem both to integrate what he had learned with the apostles' understanding of the church and to assure them that he was still faithful to the gospel. On his arrival in Jerusalem following his third missionary journey, the church expressed deep concern regarding his activities (21:17-21). Paul gives a full report in which he satisfies their concerns. His subsequent arrest is incidental to preventing a possible rift between Antioch in its concern for outreach and Jerusalem in its concern for purity.

## Unity and Diversity

Culture is not the center of the Bible; Christ is. But when the Bible mentions culture, it is important. Likewise, we must take culture and cultural differences seriously—for the sake of the life of the church.

First, in regard to organization, when the first-century Christians took culture seriously and split the power structure, acknowledging the importance of different ethnic groups (Acts 6 and 13), the church expanded. We must follow their example. We need not waste our energies trying to integrate every Bible study, for example, with one Black and one Hispanic for every eight Whites. (In fact, this could insure that the minorities would always be outvoted eight to two.) Undoubtedly there were many house churches in the first century made up entirely of one ethnic group or another.

Rather it is far more crucial to integrate the leadership in national Christian circles. How many Christian radio stations, seminaries, publishing houses, service organizations or mission agencies are honestly giving Blacks, Hispanics or Asians the opportunity to share power effectively in their organizational structures? If we insist there is no unique Black culture or Polish culture or Mexican culture, we will continue to cut them out of places of leadership. Let us recognize their importance, allow each part of the body to exercise its gifts and thus expand God's work.

Second, acknowledging the importance of culture strengthens the church by helping each individual grow in Christ. With my limitations of language and experience, I cannot fully comprehend the meditative nature of Eastern Christianity or the vibrant dynamism of Latin American evangelism or the spiritual freedom of the African mind, but by faith I can accept that Jesus Christ's manifestation of himself is far greater than I can comprehend on this earth, and I can accept all of these as brothers and sisters because our unity is found in the gospel of Jesus Christ. Why should young people have to look to Eastern pantheistic mystics for a meditative experience? Where are Eastern Christians to help us? We have failed to recognize their life as a valid Christian way. I do not have to be able to reproduce the emotion-oriented worship of many Black churches to accept them in Christ any more than I should demand that they endure my emotionless exercise in intellectual worship before they can be called Christians.

Where then is the unity of the church? We live in a world of rapid change that no Christian should fear. If we believe God to be unchanging and absolute, then the more rapidly life changes, the more visible are the unchangeables. As one culture contacts and interacts with another, we are better able to identify what unchanging universals are accepted by Christians everywhere. Today we are witnessing a worldwide council of Jerusalem in which the universals of the faith are being hammered out on the anvil of church-mission relationships. As in the book of Acts, there is much discussion, difference of opinion and direction from the Holy Spirit. We can face this "council" confidently, secure that differences will not divide us because God's revelation is complete in Christ.

The gospel incorporates all the nations and ethnic and social groups of the earth. That's what the early church discovered. Although they began with de facto segregation, the Holy Spirit began to open their eyes through miracles, through teaching, through all that they had seen Christ do. As the Holy Spirit began to open doors they walked through them, one by one, until we find the church has changed from a sect of Judaism to a universal church that included Samaritans, Ethiopians, Greeks, Asians, Romans —anybody who would come into the faith. That's the story that Luke was telling Theophilus. That's the story we have to tell the world if ever the gospel is to reach the many pockets of social and ethnic groups walled up within their own worlds, all deprived of the reconciliation provided in Jesus Christ.

# Part 2

## Communicating
## Christ
## Today

# 8
# Rural Christians in an Urban World

IN PART ONE WE SAW that when God's people take culture seriously, God's work expands and is strengthened. While culture is not everything, it does plan a crucial role—from Genesis all the way through the New Testament. If this is the biblical pattern, the obvious question then becomes, How should we be looking on culture today to expand and strengthen God's work in the world?

This chapter and the next will seek to give practical answers to this question. To begin, however, we need to consider the two thousand years of church history between the New Testament era and the present.

## Waves of History

When I was in California for a year of study at Fuller Theological Seminary, I became enamored with surfing. A great wave will loom over your head and you have to get on your board and ride the wave, or it will crush you. Once you are up, the ride is exhilarating until the wave carries you to up, the ride is exhilarating until the wave carries you to shore. Then, if you are going to surf anymore, you need to get off the board and swim out to catch the next wave.

I have seen a relationship between these phases of surfing (catching the wave, riding it, getting off) and the history of Christianity. Kenneth Scott Latourette saw Christian history as a series of pulses—periods of expansion each followed by a period of retreat. Ralph Winter has found it instructive to place a four-hundred-year grid over the last two thousand years. Figure 1 summarizes how I see the three phases of a wave applying in each segment.

**Figure 1**
**The Wave Theory of Christian History**

| Four-Hundred-Year Grid | Phase 1 Catching the Wave | Phase 2 Riding the Wave | Phase 3 Getting off the Wave |
|---|---|---|---|
| 0-400 | Early Church | Constantine | Barbaric Invasions |
| 400-800 | Barbaric Invasions | Carolingian Renaissance and | Moslem Advances |
| 800-1200 | Nordic Invasions | Alfred the Great Cluny Gregory VII | Crusades East-West Church Split |
| 1200-1600 | Mongol Invasions Friars | Plagues Corruption in Church "Babylonian Captivity" of Papacy | Early Reformers |
| 1600-2000 | Reformation | Colonialism | End of Colonialism |
| 2000- | Urbanization Rise of Technology | | |

In the first phase, a hostile culture looms over the church and threatens to crush it. But in the second phase (with one notable exception) the church captures the cultural wave and rides it so that God's work is carried forward. As that cultural wave breaks up, the church must also get off the wave or relinquish the opportunity to expand in the next period.

Now dividing history into periods like this is somewhat arbitrary. It would also be simplistic to say, for example, that there were only positive trends in Christianity from A.D. 500 to 700 and no positive trends from 700 to 900. Then, too, the peak in each period is not reached at its exact center nor is each peak as high as all the others. But the trends are there. Latourette expresses his own ap- proach this way:

> After its origin, the course of Christianity is treated by what the author deems to have been its major epochs. These, as he conceives them, are best seen as pulsations in the life of Christianity as reflected in its vigour and its influence upon the ongoing history of the race. The cri- teria which he believes to be valid for discerning these pulsations are, in the main, three—the expansion or re- cession of the territory in which Christians are to be found, the new movements issuing from Christianity, and the effect of Christianity as judged from the per- spective of mankind as a whole. Precise dates can seldom if ever be fixed for the pulsations. The lines between the eras are fuzzy. One age has a way of running over into its successor or of being foreshadowed before it is born. The eras are realities, but there are no sharp breaks be- tween then which can be identified by particular years. Advance and retreat often begin at different times in the several areas in which Christians are found and the first indications of revival are frequently seen before decline has been halted. Terminal dates are, therefore, only ap-

proximations. Yet approximate dates can be named.[1] The movements, the trends, the pulsations, the waves—however you put it—"the eras are realities," despite the difficulty in fixing dates. I will not expand on Figure 1 in detail, but allow me to give a few examples.

At the time of Christ the dominant cultural wave that threatened to crush the early church was the Roman Empire itself. But with the conversion of Emperor Constantine, the church was able to use this wave for its own expansion. Not all the results of Constantine's turnaround were positive, but on the whole the church grew.

As the Empire disintegrated, the invading barbarian soldiers came into contact with Christianity. The church was, at this time, linked with Rome and could have been destroyed by its association. But two trends thwarted the possibility. First, "the majority of the pagan invaders were fairly quickly brought to an outward adoption of Christianity and their faith was even carried beyond what, in the year 500, had been its northern borders."[2] Second, "as the structure of the Roman Empire disintegrated, invasions multiplied, wars and disorder increased, and life and property became progressively unsafe. The Church stepped into the breach and took over some of the functions for which society had been accustomed to look to the state."[3] Again the full results of these trends were mixed, but the church turned a potentially disastrous movement to its own advantage which culminated in the Carolingian Renaissance. Unfortunately, the simultaneous advances of Islam during this period overshadowed this rebirth.

The period of 1200 to 1600, however, saw the church unable to let go of former waves and ride new ones. The crusades, which weakened the Eastern church and blocked the expansion of Christianity into Islam even to this day, were just ending as this period began.[4] After this bad start, conditions worsened as the corruption within the church hierarchy grew. There were a few bright spots. First, the church was able to stamp out a variety of heresies.[5] Second, two missionary orders of the Catholic Church (the Franciscans and Dominicans) took advantage of the Mongol invasion of Eurasia to plant missions from Russia to the China Sea.[6] And third, immense Christian energies were released to build the cathedrals and universities of Europe. On the whole, though, the church failed to ride the cultural wave.

### The Retreat of the West
In reaction to this failure, the Reformers arose and were able to piggyback on the next wave of colonialism to spread the gospel even more. The ride on the top of that wave has been exhilarating, and we are still flushed with enthusiasm because of it. What many in the church do not appear to realize, however, is that the wave has come to shore. It has ended. We are in a period similar to the barbaric invasions of the shrinking Roman Empire. This is a period of withdrawal for the West and the rise of the Third World.

Ralph Winter has documented this incredible reversal, which he calls "the retreat of the West." In 1944, 99.5% of the population of the non-Western world was under the domination of the West. Just twenty-five years later only .5% was under Western control.[7] This was counterbalanced by heightened economic imperialism by the West,[8] but the control of the Third World over oil and other natural resources is reversing even this trend.

Despite the apparent end of colonialism, many still assume the Western church can and should continue to dominate the Third-World church. Instead of letting go of a cultural wave that has come to shore and getting on the next wave, they continue to try to ride a wave that is no longer there. They are stuck in the sand and won't admit it. Others in the church simply do not know which way to go.

They see the end of colonialism and the futility of trying to conserve colonial forms in the church. But they do not know where to look for alternatives.

What we need to ask now is, What is the next wave? What is the dynamic force that will be changing the world in the decades to come? What cultural movement looms overhead and threatens to crush the church which the church can catch and ride to its own advantage?

When you consider that missionaries have in the past been barbarian soldiers and Christian women taken captive by Vikings, you begin to see God's way with new eyes. Even "standard-type" missionaries like William Carey had to overcome great resistance from their own people and practically be stowaways on ships because the established church would not help them. The early part of any of these waves sees new, creative ways of getting the gospel out.

We have, for example, been used to asking governments to let in missionaries from mission agencies. But now many governments will not allow them in. Are we to forsake that country for years or possibly decades until the officials have a change of heart (or the country a change of government)?

For forty years Portugal was ruled by the facist dictator Antonio de Oliveira Salazar, who opposed both Protestantism and Communism. When a few years after his stroke in 1968, free elections were held, who was organized? The Communists. By the end of 1977 they were able to topple moderate Premier Mario Soares after only seventeen months of democratic government.

Both Communists and Protestants had been banned officially, and the Catholic Church was repressed. Despite this the Communists informally infiltrated every village. When the ban was lifted, it was a simple step to a formal organization. But where was the church? Because of the mindset that we can only work through governments, the church had little influence. There are other ways to communicate a message, as the Communists showed. We need a new mindset and new, creative ways to communicate our eternal message.

## The New Wave

We will find these new avenues in what I believe to be the overriding movements that today are affecting people on every continent around the world: urbanization and technology. Figure 2 illustrates the rapid progress of urbanization since 1800.

**Figure 2**
**Urbanization since 1800**

Percentage of World Population in Cities of 20,000 or More

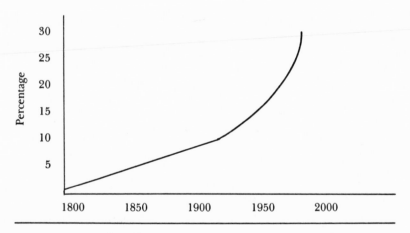

Sources: Kingsley Davis, "The Origin and Growth of Urbanization in the World," *The American Journal of Sociology*, March 1955, and United Nations, *Statistical Yearbook 1969*.

Table 1 shows that while urbanization has progressed to different levels and proceeds at different rates, nonetheless, the trend exists on every continent.

Some might object that urbanization is not occurring, that people are in fact leaving the core cities for the sub-

**Table 1**
**Urbanization from 1940-1969**

|  | Percentage of Population in Cities of 20,000 or More | | | | Percentage Change from 1940-1969 |
|---|---|---|---|---|---|
|  | 1940 | 1950 | 1960 | 1969 |  |
| World | 19 | 21 | 25 | 28 | +9 |
| Africa | 7 | 10 | 13 | 16 | +9 |
| North America | 46 | 51 | 58 | 62 | +16 |
| South America | 20 | 25 | 33 | 37 | +17 |
| Asia | 10 | 12 | 16 | 18 | +8 |
| Europe | 39 | 41 | 44 | 46 | +7 |
| Oceania | 41 | 46 | 53 | 53 | +8 |
| USSR | 24 | 28 | 36 | 42 | +18 |

Source: United Nations, *Statistical Yearbook 1969*.

urbs. While this is so in some parts of the world, in most parts urban centers are simply expanding geographically. Suburbia is still sub-urban. The overall process is a movement away from rural living.

As one might expect when you begin throwing around sociological terms, there are a variety of definitions that scholars use and argue over.

Kenneth Little distinguishes among three definitions.

The term "urbanization" has several different meanings. It frequently refers to living in towns as against living in rural settlements, and it is with this meaning in mind that simple quantitative indices of urbanization are sometimes constructed. . . . Another type of definition holds that urbanization is a process of population concentration in which the ratio of urban people to the total population in a territory increases. . . . I prefer to regard urbanization as a cultural and social psychological process. By means of this process people acquire elements of material and non-material culture—including behavioral patterns, forms of organization, and ideas—that originate in or are distinctive of the city. A corollary of this is that country persons moving to the city, or visiting it, become urbanized to the extent that they acquire urban characteristics of behavior and thought, or material objects which through possession or use affect their conduct, ideas, and social relationships. Similarly, the farm or village resident may become urbanized as the culture of the city is conveyed to the rural community and there integrated into the ideational and behavioral patterns of the residents.[9]

I want to focus my attention on the last type of urbanization Little has described—a shift in behavior patterns and in values. A rural culture is one with *a geographic frame of reference.* In Africa, a people on a plateau bounded by a river on one side and a mountain range on another and a forest on another will develop a certain culture distinct from those who live in the mountains or those in the forest. Those on the plateau have long bows because they are moving around in a large open territory. They can see danger at great distances and can plan accordingly. Those in the forest will have short bows so they can run easily and at a moment's notice. Because of the vegetation, they can only see short distances, and danger is potentially close at all times. Their whole life, you see, takes shape around the geography they live in.

In America an east-west highway will be crossed by a main street, and stores and houses will grow around the intersection. If someone drives through that geographic area, he or she has intruded on the culture. "Who is it?" "What do they want?" "What are they up to?" The culture responds to all activity, natural or supernatural, that intrudes its space. There will be functional diversity but geographic limitation.

Urban culture, by contrast, has *a functional frame of reference*. People participate in activities or respond to events not on the basis of geography but on the basis of spheres of influence. Again in contrast to rural culture, there is geographic mobility. An American steel executive can travel around the world by jet, stay in Hilton Hotels and rent Hertz cars wherever he or she goes, discuss business in person or on the phone with Japanese, German and Nigerian steel executives—and never penetrate another culture. Such people operate in a sphere of influence and out of a value system that goes with them wherever they go.

The First National Bank of Chicago says, "In 1905, we decided to organize our loan departments on the basis of the businesses and industries we loaned *to,* rather than the geographical locations we loaned *at. We organized to serve the needs of our customers.*"[10] (emphasis theirs). The bank saw seventy-five years ago that the city was not organized geographically but functionally. My hope, as will become clear in the pages to come, is that the church will begin to see the wisdom of doing the same.

## From Notched Sticks to Computer Bits

Of course urbanization does have certain geographical characteristics. In New York, for example, you have the Hudson River on one side and the East River on the other side of Manhattan. Certain sections began to develop where the boats dock; the hotel district and the warehouses, and industries and retailing developed near there. All these functions are compressed geographically and stretch up fifty stories in skyscrapers for the sake of communication.

*Communication* is the key word. "Cities were evolved primarily for the facilitation of human communication,"[11] not because geography compelled people to move closer. I recognize, of course, that here again we find ourselves in the middle of a debate among sociologists and urban specialists on urban growth and structure, or on what makes cities tick. F. Stuart Chapin, Jr. has highlighted no less than six main theories which emphasize, among others, economics, accessibility and communications as proposed keys to understanding urban activity.[12] While each theory has its merits and uses, I have found the communications approach the most adaptable to the needs of the church and the truest to my own experience. Paul Craven and Barry Wellman elaborate on this view, emphasizing the communication networks in the city and de-emphasizing geography.

> We have been careful not to define communities in spatial terms, as areas whose boundaries can be drawn on a map. In considering a community, we can just as easily be talking about a dense, bounded network of enthusiastic stamp collectors as of one of fellow residents in a particular locality. While many discussions have equated "community" with "neighborhood," we feel that it is intellectually more profitable to see the neighborhood as only a special case of community. Furthermore, *not all neighborhoods are necessarily communities;* there will be many residential localities in the city where there is little interpersonal network linkage among the inhabitants. The identification of neighborhood with community was probably more appropriate in the period before the development of widespread transportation and communication facilities; when mobility is low and communication difficult, much of one's interpersonal interaction will take place within a relatively confined geographical area.[13]

The consideration of widespread transportation and communication facilities leads us to the second major force active today—technology. Its combination with urbanization has been even more significant than it would be on its own. When cities first developed, "communication was re-stricted to face-to-face interaction but very quickly the need for records developed. Thus notched sticks, clay tablets, papyri, and smooth stone surfaces were marked with knives, styli, pens and chisels according to the local code, and communication became instrumented."[14] The next major development was the printing press. In the nine-teenth century, steamships, railroads, telegraphs, tele-phones and photographs were introduced, and the wave of technology began to rise. Television, radio, air travel, trucking, satellites and computers have all added energy to the movement in this century.

"The machinery of communication is merely a vast elab-oration of the work of the scribe and the courier, two social roles that became important to the organization of large communities at the dawn of history. Face-to-face communi-cations go back to the origins of language itself. Thus the proliferation of communications technique is a funda-mental property of urbanism."[15] While urban cultures tend to remain *functionally rigid* today as they did five thousand (or even five hundred) years ago, the chief difference is the far greater degree of *geographic mobility* made possible by the technological revolution.

I have a friend who was an executive in Borden's Milk Company. They used to buy milk from upstate New York, and then process it right in New York City and sell it to the people in the area. They started trotting the milk out at five o'clock with horses and buggies; then they got trucks. That is all gone now, of course. Today they buy their milk from anywhere in the United States, because in twenty-four hours you can fly it in or move it through the night by re-frigerated milk trucks and the like. Borden's has in fact moved out of New York almost entirely except for one of their major milk-processing plants. Their headquarters is in Ohio and its major branches are located from one coast to the other. The executive officers use computers and tele-phones to keep track of their warehousing. It is not neces-sary to see face to face the people that they are dealing with.

Another example comes from Kenya. Right after inde-pendence a million-and-a-half Africans were resettled onto the old European farms. They were each given seven acres. Traditional African culture would have demanded that they move their families onto those seven acres and plow them. But they did not. They organized into groups of farms with movable fences that were simple slats of wood tied together. Then they hired a tractor to plow all the fields. Next they arranged for a trucker with a fleet of Peugot station wagons to bring them seed from the city for the cash crop they grow, seed which the farmers purchased on credit. After putting their fences back up, they all plant-ed. At harvest time the fences came back down and the families hired someone else to harvest the whole plot. Truckers then took the crop to market. Those who plowed, harvested and trucked the seed and the crop all took their cut from the cooperative. These families are one-hundred-and-twenty miles from Nairobi and have no education. But they are as urbanized as Borden's because their life is dominated by a functional frame of reference and not a geographical one.

I have another friend who raises cattle in Kansas. At first we might say he is rural since his nearest neighbor is eight miles away. But consider how he does business. He buys thousands of head at one time from breeders in Texas when the cattle are three months old. He then fattens them for a few months and sells them. That's all he does. It is his whole business. If he is forced to sell them three days too late, his whole profit is lost. How does he know when to buy and when to sell?

First, he is in constant contact with the big breeders in Texas. Then he has an agent in Chicago buying grain for him. By watching *The Chicago Tribune* every day he can figure the cost of grain per pound of meat and calculate the date of sale. Finally he keeps in touch with buyers in Iowa who will complete the fattening process before slaughter. He is on the phone constantly. He even has a small airplane so he can be in Texas and Chicago regularly.

Is this rural America? He does not know his neighbors. Why? His neighbor raises poultry. My friend's whole life is beef. His entire social, economic and political relationships revolve around the beef industry. The people he goes to dinner with, the people he socializes with, the people he goes to the theater with are all connected to the beef industry in Chicago or in Texas or in Kansas.

I asked him if he went to church. "Well, I've been to church in Wichita, about twenty-five miles away." He is not too interested in the people in Kansas, however—other than those in the beef industry. So how is the church going to function effectively in that kind of context?

Consider the people who live in high-rise apartments. They are as difficult to reach as those in the ghetto. It is pointless to suggest one do door-to-door evangelism in a high rise because the people who live there are buying protection from any stranger who might knock on their door. If you do knock, you are their enemy. The first thing they will do is call the guard and say, "How did this creep get in here? Get him out!" They have locks on their doors; they have guards; they have phone systems; they have two-way radios that communicate up and down. You ring the buzzer and the buzzer says, "Who is it?" They do not want you in and they pay big money to keep you out. They did not choose a high rise so they could be close to lots of other people, but so they could be separated.

The kind of housing you select in the city is determined by the kind of values you have already selected, unless you are one of the oppressed. To come into a ghetto and start talking about building a neighborhood church will achieve little since there is no neighborhood. If people are not functioning on geographical lines, the church is not going to function on geographical lines either.

Even in suburbia, how many people know everyone on their block? How many have best friends whom they got to know because they lived in their neighborhood? Communication is possible over a much wider geographic area with those whose values are more similar than those who live next door. So we do not talk to our neighbors but to those in our profession, in our family, in our volunteer groups—who may be scattered across the city or state or nation.

The rise of urbanism has profound implications for us in the church in the West and especially in America, because, for the most part, we in the church have a rural, geographic mindset. Foreign missions to most of us means ministry thousands of miles away, not ten miles away in the Puerto Rican district. Door-to-door evangelism dominates the witness of many groups. The changes in the church in the coming years will necessarily be substantial. I do not know precisely what forms the church will use to spread the Christian message in an urbanized world, but I hope in the next chapters to draw the broad outlines within which I believe we should work.

**In Two Worlds**
Let me close this chapter with the story of Bill, a Christian business executive with Standard Oil in Chicago. His work took him around the world, including Kenya where I met him. One time he was playing golf in Kenya alone and decided to pair up with another man who was also alone. They teed off and began to chat. In the middle of the game Bill asked his partner what he did for a living. "I'm a missionary," came the reply. Bill stopped suddenly and stared in

shock. Moments later he began to weep.

His home church had sent two missionaries to Kenya. Bill had been to Nairobi three times. It had never occurred to him that he was on the mission field. He traveled to Saudi Arabia and to Kenya and back home and never left his culture. His mind functioned entirely along business channels. Yet fifteen miles from where he stood on that golf course was a missionary his church supported named Maria. For the first time in thirty-five years of being a "rural" Christian and twenty-five years of being an "urban" businessman, his two worlds crashed together and Bill could not cope.

The two of them did not finish the golf game. They picked up their balls and went to visit the missionary his church supported. When he met Maria, Bill got so excited and was in such culture shock that he bought her $250 in gifts. For a day and a half all he could say was how funny it was that he was on the mission field.

We in the church in the West are like Bill. We are simultaneously in two worlds. We can pretend that one world is not waning and strain to hold on to it; or we can be suddenly shocked into an awareness of the new coming era. We can be paralyzed by fear of the wave of urbanization and technology that is coming upon us. Or we can seek out creative new means of dealing with these movements as Christians throughout the centuries have done. I do not know exactly what these new ideas will look like, but I believe they are there to be found by courageous Christians willing to try. We can, we must take advantage of those forces that threaten to destroy us and use them to expand and strengthen God's church.

# 9
## Networks of Communication

URBANISM IS A DYNAMIC multidimensional array of human communication networks. But our rural mindset blinds us to the importance of these. Rather, our orientation is toward impersonal power structures and institutions. These are really what matter, aren't they?

Russell Hitt, author and former editor of *Eternity* magazine, provides us with a striking illustration of this kind of thinking in an *Eternity* article entitled "New York City: Spiritual Power Failure."[1] This was part of "Evangelicals in America," a series of articles focusing on different sections of the country. I respect Hitt and believe he did a remarkable job, considering his limited sources and the deadlines involved in putting out a magazine. But his article betrays a one-dimensional perspective.

**Power Structures and Human Networks**
He begins with people, but his choice is telling. "The Big

Apple . . . is worm-ridden on the inside with muggers and dope peddlers, Mafia capos, and slimy politicians." As soon as he introduces power structures, the change is startling. "With all its filth and crime and political corruption, it still remains the most powerful city in the world. It is the capital of the U.S. world of finance, communication, book and magazine publishing, and the garment industry. It's the nation's richest port. There is only one Wall Street, one Broadway, one Fifth Avenue lined with smart shops like Tiffany and Cartier. Not far away from Central Park and the Plaza Hotel is Bloomingdales, mecca of ecstatic shoppers. Gleaming skyscrapers house the offices of the conglomerates and multi-national corporations."

The positiveness with which he approaches these institutions all in the heart of the downtown area, is apparent. But when he talks about people and the human networks of communication, he mentions only those in another part of the city, not in the downtown area. These he sees negatively. This underlying value system places worth in the power structures. The communication networks among the people are secondary at best.

Then he switches from power structures back to people. "The ethnic and religious complexity of New York is staggering. It is, for example, the largest Jewish city in the world. . . . Of the 1.7 million Puerto Ricans living on the U.S. mainland, half live in New York, especially in East Harlem, the South Bronx and enclaves of Brooklyn. Here is found the largest black population of any city of the United States, congregated largely in Harlem and the Bedford-Stuyvesant section of Brooklyn and Newark. Blacks make up 25% of the population in Manhattan, the Bronx and Brooklyn which compares to 11% of the general U.S. population." It is not Hitt's fault that negative images jump into the minds of most Americans when they hear about 1.7 million Puerto Ricans and Blacks in the Bronx and Brooklyn. But he goes on to give his perspective on this situation which reveals his own myopia. "One has to search for vital Christianity," because we don't expect it among 1.7 million Puerto Ricans. "And yet it can be found —in unlikely places." Again, value and worth; according to a rural mindset, should be found in the institutions, not among the people.

He returns to power structures when he mentions the Billy Graham Crusade in Madison Square Garden. He institutionalizes Billy Graham—and not Billy Graham in Manhattan, but Billy Graham in the institution of Madison Square Garden. "The next time Billy Graham conducts a crusade in Madison Square Garden, he'll probably have to speak in Spanish. Besides its huge Puerto Rican population, other Hispanic groups are pouring into New York, legally and illegally."

Unfortunately, Russell Hitt is mistaken. Billy Graham will never speak in Spanish in New York because Billy Graham has been there three times in the last fifteen years and few who are Spanish come because most do not know he is there. The auditorium will be filled with twenty thousand suburbanites who drive into the city. They are the ones who know Graham is there, and they come to see him. There is this vast difference between the structural approach to the city, which is a top-down approach, and the people approach. Hitt is vaguely aware that this difference exists, but he has not seen the degree to which the structural approach misses the people of the city.

He continues to consider the church from a structural perspective. "The once great Protestant churches of Manhattan and Brooklyn gradually are disappearing. . . . Yet there are some surprising bright spots. . . . There are still some strong conservative churches like the Fifth Avenue and Madison Avenue Presbyterian Churches and near Columbia University Broadway Presbyterian that ministers to the academic community." It is difficult to relate that paragraph to people. He has not mentioned the name of the pastor; he rarely mentions what kind of people attend there. He has simply mentioned that these are the going churches. The city is such a spiritually dark quarter, however, that even establishment churches with a little life are called "surprising bright spots."

The sentences which follow in the article focus on more institutions: Norman Vincent Peale's Marble Collegiate Church (another institutionalized person), Calvary Baptist Church on 57th Street, New York Theological Seminary, "the huge Protestant center at 475 Riverside Drive, headquarters for the National Council of Churches and many major Protestant denominations. Nearby is theologically liberal Union Theological Seminary." In doing this, Hitt is communicating a whole way of viewing life and what is important. The overall picture is a dreary one because the institutions of the church, its power structures, have come on hard times and are on the way out.

The picture changes, as does the whole tone of the article, when Hitt begins to focus on the unexpected human networks that are on the way up.

The sovereign grace of God is not thwarted by the migration of believers to the suburbs. In the Puerto Rican and Hispanic barrios of East Harlem and the Bronx, there are literally scores of storefront churches led by obscure but faithful men of God who are preaching the gospel of love. . . . There is a quality to the Spanish-language churches that is light miles above traditional Protestantism. The ebullient Hispanic people not only preach the gospel, they demonstrate their love for fellow members to those outside that recalls the infant church of Acts. . . . They share their possessions. . . . Many of these little churches surround new immigrants with a love that is matched by their obedience to the law. . . .

*140*

There are many eloquent black preachers. Dr. Gardner C. Taylor, leader of the Progressive Baptists, who serves a flock of 12,000 at Concord Baptist Church in Brooklyn, is an outstanding illustration. . . . The stones cry out in another unexpected quarter—the number of Jews who are acclaiming Jesus Christ as their true Messiah.

The tone is suddenly bright and alive—*quality, ebullient, demonstrate their love, share their possessions, eloquent black preachers, serves a flock, outstanding.* He does not emphasize buildings or streets. He speaks of powerful leadership and faithful men.

In this article, I believe Hitt has viewed the city and the church in the city the way most in the middle class do—as institutions. When he discovers that there is a vital church out among the people, it amazes him. Even so it is clear that he has not understood that some of the institutional churches he names are doing little that affects the city. They are two-thirds empty; the people who do attend are elderly; and even their money is drying up. Because he is not plugged into the human communication networks but deals primarily with establishment power structures, he has completely missed a five-thousand member church whose leadership has started a two-thousand member subchurch and is now planning five other new churches.

Bishop Brown started an independent Pentecostal church in the Bronx with a membership of twelve hundred and set up Bible-school training for all of his people, six nights a week. Out of that has developed a leadership class that runs the church and a group of young preachers. They have planted eleven churches in New York—all of them with a membership of more than two hundred. They have $1.6 million of property under their control. They have four hundred eighty people registered in their school which has grown from a one-year basic course for all new Christians to a three-year curriculum of Bible study. They also offer a one-year advanced Bible-training course and a doctrinal course for those who want to become pastoral ministers. A five-year Bible school that meets six nights a week is not unusual. There are at least ten similar schools in the Black community alone in New York.

Where is the church in the city? We do not see it, because we are oriented toward the power structures and see only emptiness and decay, and conclude the church is dead. When we are among the people and begin to see their experience and the strength in their leadership, we see that there is vitality. The church is alive and growing and dynamic in the city.

In chapter eight I briefly mentioned the main lines of communication that run through our urban world. I like to think of these as cultural stripes which cut across broad geographic areas. In the remainder of this chapter we will look at four primary categories of these networks (government, professions, kinship and volunteer associations), and in chapter ten we will explore one more—ethnicity. Through these cultural stripes we will be better able to see the nature of human relationships today.

## Government: More Than Bureaucracy
One of the basic ways we understand the city is as a political unit. From a communications perspective, we can see the city as a group of administrative responsibilities, as Amos Hawley does in *Urban Society: An Ecological Approach.*[2] Administration is simply one way to communicate. When you see a plow outside in the snow, you know somebody told the driver in the plow to get out and clear the streets. The driver's boss told him to get the plow out, and so on until you come to the person who has final administrative responsibility. In other words, nothing happens by accident.

We would be misled, however, if we thought that the only communication in government comes down from the top of the administrative pyramid and occasionally goes back up. American cities, especially, were not planned. They were formed haphazardly. Often, therefore, administrations will not respond to their own system but will react to other influences such as interest groups.

For instance, I found two Christian teachers in a public school system in Newark. Assuming that there were also some Christian children in the system, we turned loose two summer volunteers in our urban outreach ministry to canvass the neighborhood to find out where the children went to church. In that canvass we uncovered eight or ten Christian homes that were concerned with the school. They represented three or four churches who had an impact on another thirty or forty children in their Sunday schools. So we began with fifty school children, eight parents, two teachers and three churches.

Next we got the parents together in a small prayer group with the teachers. As a result, they developed a child-evangelism type of program, but with neighborhood parents and neighborhood teachers working together in the neighborhoods.

Later, we recruited another Christian from outside the system to apply for a job at that school. We also encouraged two of the parents to get into the P.T.A. and extended our influence there.

The fifty children, of course, reported to their parents about what was happening in school. So we were able as a group to keep close tabs on problems as they developed and respond effectively to them. For instance, we discovered that two Muslims in the school were pushing their theology on the kids. Of course when we raised some questions about this, they in turn raised some questions about our prayer group. Eventually, however, the Muslims got uncomfortable. They saw that they were not going to accomplish anything in that school system; so they left.

*143*

After this two other Christian teachers who had been hiding in the woodwork began to identify with the prayer group. Then we were joined by two other teachers, one Black and one White, who were not religious conservatives but who were concerned for the good of the children. They recognized that this was the body of people that was doing the most for the school. So they got on the bandwagon.

Quite unexpectedly, we then had a change in the administration. A new principal was brought in from the outside, and nobody knew who she was. As it turned out, she was a Christian who was excited about working in the system and was very supportive of the prayer group. Now we had a neighborhood school that was beginning to provide solid education. It was not the best education; it was still part of the Newark school system. It was full of.all kinds of problems. But you see that here was a government system we could affect positively by ignoring the board of education and looking to the lines of communication that naturally existed in the city.

### Professions: Opening Closed Circles
Another functional culture is the professions. The medical, legal, ministerial, military, governmental, academic and entertainment professions are all cultural stripes that transcend geographic limitations. On the other hand, professional people are not so mobile that they can walk into a ghetto. They are functionally restricted.

In fact, it is easier for one doctor to communicate with another doctor than it is for the doctor to communicate with a schoolteacher. That is what you see when you attend a P.T.A. meeting. Parents cannot communicate because union workers do not know how to communicate to doctors about the school system. Union workers can go to doctors for checkups. But they cannot talk about the local school system together because their value bases are being isolated more and more from each other.

William Goode of Columbia University highlights the following eight characteristics of a professional community. (1) Its members are bound by a sense of identity. (2) Once in it, few leave, so that it is a terminal or continuing status for the most part. (3) Its members share values in common. (4) Its role definitions *vis-à-vis* both members and non-members are agreed upon and are the same for all members. (5) Within the areas of communal action there is a common language, which is understood only partially by outsiders. (6) The Community has power over its members. (7) Its limits are reasonably clear, though they are not physical and geographical, but social. (8) Though it does not produce the next generation biologically, it does so socially through its control over the selection of professional trainees, and through its training processes it sends these recruits through an adult socialization process. Of course, professions vary in the degree to which they are communities, and it is not novel to view them as such.[3]

If you want to be a doctor today, you have to determine it before you get into high school, because you have to take college preparatory courses in high school that will get you into an elite premedical school. Then, once in medical school, you have to agree to be a part of that system. I have probed this with medical students in Inter-Varsity Christian Fellowship. They are essentially being told what kind of car they can buy, what kind of games they can play, what kind of neighborhood they can live in. They have to demonstrate through their style of living a willingness to sell themselves to the system. If they don't, it will be very difficult for them to get their degree. The social pressures to conform, though often subtle, are tremendous. Social ostracism and harassment in school work or internships are real, if unconsciously used, weapons which aim to push

renegades out or make them toe the line. Some can with-
stand the pressures. Others cannot. It is the same in the
legal profession.

Professional sports are the same. If you are going to be a
professional athlete, you will know it when you are in the
eighth grade because you will be the superhero. You will
be the quarterback on the high-school football team because you will be the best. When you get to college, you
are going to make the first string in your first or second
year. If you inherently have the quality that is going to make
you a professional, it will be obvious back in the seventh or
eighth grade. So all through high school and college you
will develop a superior attitude that says, "Everybody worships me." This is then fostered by the profession itself with
its pomp, grandeur and hero worship. If you refuse that
style of life and those values, just as if you refuse to drive a
Mercedes (and all the values that go with it) in the medical
profession, you will be ostracized.

This is precisely what happened to Roger Maris after
he broke Babe Ruth's record for home runs in one season.
He decided he did not want to go along with the hero-
worship system; he just wanted to play baseball. Maris himself said, "All I was trying to do was my job. I played from
1961 to 1968 with people on my ass in every ball park in the
country. I don't know how it got started, I'd look in the
paper and see myself described as 'sullen' and 'arrogant'
and 'surly.' I mean, take this whole temperament thing.
The fans and writers wanted me to be Babe Ruth all over
again. Well, I never wanted to be Babe Ruth in the first
place. What did they want from me...? To go down
Broadway with 10 dames on my arm and stand on street
corners eating hot dogs by the dozen? No, it was never any
fun after I hit those 61 homers. . . . I know what happened
back there. I know how the system used me; that's what I
know, and nothing will ever change it. You can call it bit-

terness if you want. I don't think so." Maris quit baseball early, just after turning thirty-four, a drained and broken man because he would not abide by the rules of his profession. He refused to be a superhero, and it destroyed what was left of his career.

Our concern as Christians should also go beyond the issues of individual lifestyle to larger issues. Who will be deciding when old people will be allowed to die? Who will be making recommendations on abortion? The doctors. Who will be ruling on issues of freedom of religion? The judges. One of the main channels of power in our urbanized world are the professions.

How do we infiltrate these lines of communication for Christ? We do what missionaries have been doing for years. We learn the language. We get to know key individuals who can then communicate even more effectively to their peers, and suddenly we have a church.

We could be misled if we viewed the task solely from a structural perspective. There is more to the medical profession than the A.M.A., more to the legal profession than the American Bar Association. We should focus on the communication networks rather than on the organizational structures.

There was a time when conservative Christians said, "You can't be a professional baseball player and a Christian because they play on Sunday." So for years those in baseball and other sports did not hear the gospel. Then the Fellowship of Christian Athletes (FCA) organized to penetrate that cultural system for Christ. They brought the church to the people instead of making the people come to the church. When the gospel was communicated to the athletes in a language and a context that they could understand, they responded. The result? Most teams have Sunday chapel in the locker room. Many have even hired chaplains. It is not uncommon to hear a quarterback give God credit for his gifts on nationally televised interviews. FCA probably has more to do in helping these athletes relate to the Christian church at large, but FCA certainly has begun by moving in the right direction.

My question now is, who will penetrate rodeos, opera, the circus? Why are these groups so patently unchristian? Because the Christians are not there. Who will be the missionaries who will penetrate not unreached lands, but unreached value systems? People are already doing it in the world of professional skiing.[4]

Government circles are also starting to be reached. Many prayer fellowships have developed in Washington over the past few years. And now they are starting to pop up all over the world. Why? Because Ethiopian leaders can communicate more easily to American Congressional representatives than to Ethiopian peasants just outside Addis Ababa. Why? The concerns and priorities of government leaders are the same around the world. How do you spend this money? How do you solve that transportation problem? How do you resolve that international conflict?

As important as the local church is, we must not forget that it is a human network of communication. The church is not ultimately an organization or an institution or a building or a ministry. It is the fellowship of all believers wherever they may be. Let us, therefore, bring the professions into the church.

### Kinship: Family and the Family of God

The third major communication network is kinship. This is distinguished from ethnicity, which I take up in the next chapter, in that kinship concerns one's extended family (cousins, uncles, grandparents, and so on) while ethnicity concerns larger racial groupings (Poles, Hispanics, Chinese, and so on). They are, of course, related in that kinship is the backbone of communication in any ethnic community. While we generally acknowledge that the White, middle-class family is deteriorating, our stereotype of Black families is an even bleaker one: the father never home, the children on the streets all night. But if you measure family strength by the extended family rather than the nuclear family, by the ability of a wide range of relatives to live harmoniously under one roof, then the Black family is stronger than the White family. Kinship, therefore, remains a strong force in areas where ethnicity is strong.

Kinship is, in fact, one of the key funnels in the movement to the city. Most people do not go to a city in which they know no one and start looking for a house. Rather, they go to the city of a brother, a cousin or a distant uncle who can put them up for a while and help them find housing. Often, then, you will find Black churches in Philadelphia relating regularly with people in Mississippi or Georgia but not with Black Christians in Pittsburgh. The kinship lines go south. The need to survive in the city can, therefore, draw family connections even tighter.

I used a slogan during my four years of ministry in Newark: Every person is a doorway to a family, and every family is a gateway to a community. I would start all kinds of ministries by simply saying to the staff that worked under me, "Go into the streets and find any way you can to build trust with an individual. That becomes your program. Once you have developed trust with that individual, look for opportunities to communicate the gospel, but do not get all hung up on that. Try to get beyond that individual into their family relationships. In other words, if you are playing basketball in the afternoon with a young guy, and he takes to you and you like him, offer to drive him home. Find out if you can get an opportunity to stop by and visit him in his house and meet his parents."

I have found out that in an amazing way this counteracts

what has evidently been one of the greatest problems in the communication of the gospel in the city. Untold Christian organizations, including local churches, will involve themselves in the lives of young people and never take time to communicate with their families. Pretty soon families are refusing to allow their children to be involved with Christian groups. I have come across good Christian parents who are doing this simply because they do not know or understand who their kids are hanging out with.

Young Life has developed a training program for urban workers that stresses this. If you go to a high school and meet a student, spend a few weeks hanging out with him or her in various places. By the third time you meet him, make sure you meet the parents. Otherwise the parents are going to develop a block against you. The same is true for those reaching out to urban commuter campuses. You cannot form a group that is independent of family ties. You must trace the kinship lines back to have an effective campus ministry.

In an urban, commuter college setting, students maintain strong ties to the community they come from—for example, to their jobs or their families. This contrasts to the residential campus in which college is a student's whole life. Therefore, it is relatively easy to reach these students through a campus organization. But if one is to successfully influence urban, commuter students, one must be willing to follow their lines of communication back to their community base.

It is easy to initiate contact with an individual in an urban setting. But moving from the individual to the family is a difficult process. Much of it has to do with our built-in stereotypes, our built-in racism and our inherent reluctance to get involved with the problems of the city. I would suggest that if you want to get involved in an urban ministry, getting involved with an urban family is a process you need to go through yourself before you start giving direction to anyone else.

As you approach a family, it is helpful to see that most families have at least three communities in the city which influence them. Sometimes these may be geographical communities, but often they are not. First is the community of the parents' work. Second is the social community with which the family will be involved. It may be a volunteer association or the corner bar. Third is a church community. It may take a theological stance that you are not comfortable with, but you have to take it into consideration because urban families are often deeply rooted in their churches.

Because one cannot deal with a family or an individual in isolation from the other forces that are at work on them, you need to know who and what are influencing them. I would even suggest getting involved with their church community. In other words, if you want to disagree publicly with the teaching of their present church community, you had better do it from a basis of trust. You have to know the family well enough to say, "Having visited your church, I want to raise some questions about what they are teaching." But if you stand off on the outside and begin to condemn the church, you are rejecting the community of which this person is a part. Their conclusion will be that you are rejecting them too.

Some people criticize urban churches for being too social. But many middle-class Whites are also wrapped up in the church because it is their social life. People use the church as a volunteer association. In many urban (and suburban) churches, people attend for years and never get any Bible teaching. That does not necessarily mean they must leave that church. It may mean we will have to work in it.

In Newark, when I would start teaching a neighborhood Bible study on Tuesday or Thursday night, we would get all kinds of people. Sometimes they would be involved for a year before they really understood the gospel. After coming to know the Lord, they would stay involved for another year or two before suddenly raising the question, "You know, maybe this church that I'm going to isn't the one where I belong." Then they would say, "But if I pull out, where am I going to go to socialize? All my friends are at church." The church in the city can replace both kinship and volunteer associations. Because the city is an impersonal place, people need a home ground that they can come to. They will find it in the bingo hall or on a baseball team or in a church. We should, therefore, be careful about calling people out of a church.

The responsibility for in-depth follow-through is seen vividly in the story of Walter, a fourteen-year-old with whom we got involved in Newark. We found that he was staying with his aunt for the summer though his home was Mississippi. His aunt was not satisfied with the church she attended but was impressed with what happened to her nephew through our program. So she came to an adult Bible study and began to appreciate what our church was doing. She even encouraged Walter to go to our Sunday school. She returned to her own church because of established social relationships, but was also able to help start a Bible study during the week.

By the end of the summer Walter's older sister Barbara came up from Mississippi to visit. After being with her younger brother for a few hours she turned to her aunt and said, "What happened to this kid? His whole life has changed." So the aunt said, "There's a group of kids in this neighborhood that introduced him to some new thinking, and now he's a Christian." Barbara had to find out who these people were. Soon she was having a long talk with one of the girls on our team, a student from Massachusetts, who told Barbara, "I want to keep in touch with you. Give me your name and address."

We had contacts in Mississippi. So we wrote to ask a friend to just give this girl a call. He called up Barbara, and it nearly blew her off the earth. Somebody in Mississippi called her up and said, "This girl you met in Newark was concerned enough to tell me about you and I want to be in touch." This so impressed Barbara that she spent a whole weekend in Massachusetts and came to know the Lord. She went back and led her whole family to the Lord in Mississippi.

Our ministry was partly in Mississippi that summer because that is the way communications flow in the Black community. And on that block, the only one we were able to touch was Walter, a visitor from Mississippi. Following through on that network opened a ministry that was for the Lord's glory that summer.

### Volunteer Associations: Pizza Parlor Evangelism

While the movement to the city is often along kinship lines, it can also be a movement away from the family. In other words, some people come to the city because they have decided to break with their primary family. If they are successful, they will also tend to move away from kinship contacts in general. The communication network that replaces the family will often be volunteer associations.

A volunteer association is a group that is born and organized around an activity that people participate in because they want to. It can be social; it can be political; it can be economic. I am using the term more broadly than in the sense of "a Red Cross volunteer." Ethnicity is not voluntary though there are many clubs created around ethnicity. Neither is age nor sex. The YWCA, Lions Club, Union Hall, a hospital volunteer association, country clubs, athletic clubs, the Masons, business clubs, senior citizen's groups—all of these are volunteer associations. In the city of Reading, Pennsylvania (population 80,000), I have identified over three hundred such groups.

Many of these groups were established by rural-minded people who came to the city, felt uncomfortable there and developed associations that would help them to adjust. Many downtown churches have performed the same function. They have become protective groups of people with little outreach because the very need out of which they have been created thwarts outreach.

Other volunteer associations are organized either for economic benefit, for developing a power base, or to get a job done. Their concern is to organize against outside forces. Unions, street gangs, burial associations, neighborhood coalitions or cooperatives fall into this category.

Understanding volunteer associations is very important to the body of Christ because these are the groups of people with whom we are often in competition. When we call people to Jesus Christ, we may also be calling them out of the bowling league. We need to be able to provide them with more than the bowling league does.

Yet as Christians over the centuries used forces which threatened to destroy the church to expand its influence, we too can use volunteer associations to spread the gospel. We can join such groups and communicate the gospel there. Many people who are open to the gospel do not have time to talk anywhere else, but would have time to talk in a bingo hall or a bowling alley.

Joining just a few groups will make our time most effective. We can make our selection by doing two things: first, keep our own interests in mind; and second, look for the strategic centers of communication. If you like politics, join one of the major parties or a citizens' group. If you are an athletic person, join a tennis club or a handball league.

I personally happen to like food, so I joined an Italian pizza club, Victor Emmanuel II in Reading. I paid five dollars to get in, and I had to wait four weeks for my membership to clear. My last name is Hopler, you see. They finally cleared it, mainly because I'm White. (I have never seen a Black face in the whole organization.) I was aware of that. But I got into it just to see how it operates. Every Sunday afternoon a group of Italians get together for terrific Italian food. You can buy a pizza for 90¢ if you belong to the club. You have to show your card at the door, then they let you through. There's a second door which has a two-way mirror, and you stand out there while the guy inside looks you over. He then unlocks the second door, and you come into a lobby where you are grilled with all sorts of questions. Finally they let you come in and buy your pizza. That's culture. That's a private association—a channel for fellowship.

One day I got a concerned phone call saying that nobody should come next Sunday because they found a bomb in the kitchen (seven sticks of dynamite). The Mafia must be in there somewhere. I'm just a member, but it's interesting to get even that close to the internal operation. The next Sunday afternoon Anthony's Bar and Grill on 8th Street (which is just a block from my home) blew up. The Sunday after that four buildings on Cotton Street owned by another Italian were blown off the map. Now it was apparent that something was going on in the Italian community in Reading. There was nothing in the newspaper except mention of a fire here and a burning there. But I knew something was happening in the Italian community because I belonged to Victor Emmanuel II where I could buy my pizza cheaper than anywhere else.[5]

# 10
## Dynamic
## Ethnicity

I HAVE A FRIEND WHO IS a professor in UCLA's graduate program in education, working with doctoral candidates. His students will go on to train teachers at a variety of schools. One day his daughter came home from school and reported what her teacher had taught that day.

"Well, I'm sorry, dear," came his response, "but I'm afraid your teacher is wrong about that."

"What do you mean, my teacher's wrong?" And she proceeded to argue the matter with her father.

Finally he stopped her and said, "Daughter, don't you realize that I'm the person who teaches the people who teach your teachers? So how in the world can I be wrong and your teacher be right?"

"Well," came her answer, "I don't know. I'll have to ask my teacher about that."

I have had similar experiences with my own children. They latch onto something they hear at school and reject my authority or opinion. Part of the thrust of American education has been to forget one's past and become part of the new America. There continues to be great pressure, or heat, to melt us into a uniform culture in America. Those in power have purposefully (I do not say consciously) attempted to keep the country from fragmenting into its many component parts. If the country is to survive, so the argument goes, it has to have some basis for unity.

The United States is unique in the world in this regard. While Canada has been influenced primarily by the British and French, and South Africa by the British, Dutch and Indians, no other country has absorbed so many from such a variety of countries. Ethnicity, then, represents the fifth and final major category of lines of communication that cut across geographic borders, the first four being government, professions, kinship and volunteer associations.

Americans have come to regard their ethnic origins with increasing respect. Much of this increase is, I believe, related to the retreat of the West and the rise of the Third World out of colonialism. It is apparently becoming less of a problem not to be Anglo-Saxon. Yet even the way I phrased that last sentence betrays a breakdown in the melting-pot myth. All our races and cultures and values and ideas do not melt into a smooth, even, well-balanced mixture. The taste of Northern European Protestantism dominates the soup. How did this come about?

## The Making of America
America's value system was formed in a dynamic relationship with the waves of immigrants that came to this country. Some groups have had greater impact on the culture than others. The impact of each group, in my view, has been determined by a combination of at least five factors.

1. *Chronology.* The earlier a group came to the country, the greater its impact on the value system is likely to have

been since fewer values were already fixed. The English came first and so had the greatest impact. (This is reflected in Table 2.) Any groups which followed were first required to interact with an already established culture. Other Northern European Protestant groups, notably the Germans, came in great numbers after the English.

That leads to the second factor.

**Table 2**
**Distribution of White Population in the United States in 1790**

| Nationality | Number | Per Cent |
|---|---|---|
| English | 2,605,699 | 82.1 |
| Scotch | 221,562 | 7.0 |
| German | 176,407 | 5.6 |
| Dutch | 78,959 | 2.5 |
| Irish | 61,534 | 1.9 |
| French | 17,619 | .6 |
| Others | 10,664 | .3 |
| TOTAL | 3,172,444 | 100.0 |

Source: Samuel P. Orth. *Our Foreigners* (New Haven: Yale University Press, 1920).

2. *Number.* Although a group may have been represented early in the history of the United States, if a significant number did not immigrate, its impact would be small.

3. *Length of Peak.* Not only did Northern European Catholics arrive after their Protestant counterparts, their peak in immigration lasted almost fifty years compared to Eastern Europeans whose peak period was about 1915-35.

4. *Shock.* Riots and unionization are examples of highly visible events which raised the country's awareness of different groups and forced it to take their concerns into account.

5. *Push/Pull.* Generally it is held that the greater the pull

a group has felt toward America (a promise of quick wealth, for example), the easier it is for that group to integrate. If the push of a group out of their homeland dominates their decision to move (famine or religious persecution, for example), they will integrate less easily. On the whole, the easier the integration process is for a people, the greater will be their impact on the culture as a whole.

Figure 3 shows that Northern Protestant Europe has always dominated immigration to the United States, primarily by the English and the Germans. They came first; they came in the largest numbers; their peak lasted the longest. The next large group was the Northern European Catholics which included the Dutch and the French. But the main representative of this group was the Irish. Over three million Irish came in the years 1841-90, almost a million between 1851-60.[1] Irish riots also broke out in both New York and Boston. Their Catholicism was suspect, but they made their mark and became part of the value system. Today Irish policemen and politicians are highly visible in New York, Boston and Chicago. Nonetheless, Catholicism has had such negative connotations in the country as a whole that only twice has a major party nominated a Catholic for president.

Beginning in the 1880s the next two groups came—the Southern Europeans and the Eastern Europeans, including Russia. Although the latter group was larger, the former seems to have made a greater impact. The Eastern Europeans were split among many national groups while the immigration of Southern Europeans was dominated by Italians who came in greater numbers than either Russians or Poles (see Figure 4). In fact, over three million Italians came between 1901 and 1920.[2] Today we still hear a lot of Italian and Polish jokes, more in the North than in the South. These arise out of a need to keep people in their places, to indicate that we each have our station in society.

**Figure 3**
**Foreign-Born Population of the United States: 1850-1970**
**(figures in millions)**

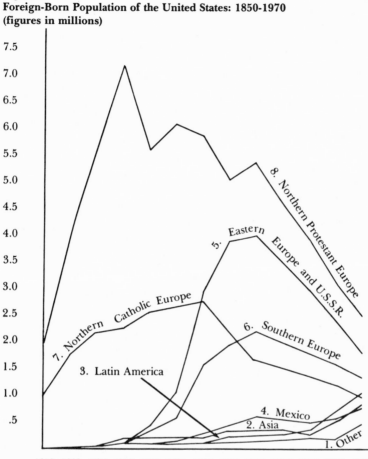

Source: U.S. Bureau of Census, *Historical Statistics of the United States: Colonial Times to 1970*, Bicentennial Edition, Part I, Washington, D.C., 1975.
Note: No figures available for 1940. For 1950 figures available only for Mexico, Asia and Other.
Key: 8 = *Northern Protestant Europe*—England, Scotland, Wales, Northern Ireland (1930-70 only), Norway, Sweden, Denmark, Iceland, Netherlands, Luxembourg, Switzerland, Germany, British Canada (estimated for 1850-80 and 1960-70).
    7 = *Northern Catholic Europe*—Ireland, Belgium, France, Austria, French Canada (estimated for 1850-80 and 1960-70).
    6 = *Southern Europe*—Albania, Greece, Italy, Portugal, Spain.
    5 = *Eastern Europe and U.S.S.R.*—Poland, Czechoslovakia, Hungary, Yugoslavia, U.S.S.R., Latvia, Estonia, Lithuania, Finland, Romania, Bulgaria, Turkey in Europe.
    4 = *Mexico*.
    3 = *Latin America*—Cuba, West Indies, Central America, South America.
    2 = *Asia*—Armenia, Palestine, Syria, Turkey in Asia, China, Japan, India, Korea, Philippines, Other Asia.
    1 = *Other*—Africa, Australia, Azores, Other Atlantic Islands, Pacific Islands, Country not Specified, Born at Sea.

**Figure 4**
**Foreign-Born Population of Most Visible Groups in the United States: 1850-1970**
**(figures in millions)**

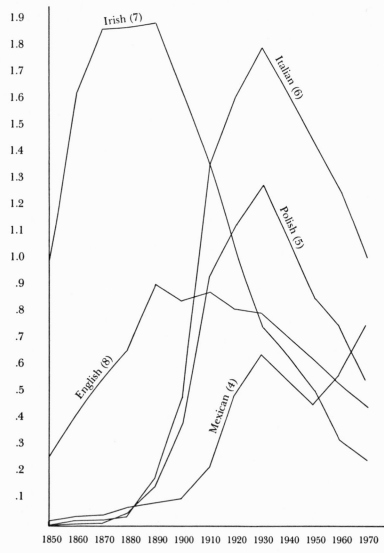

Source: U.S. Bureau of Census, *Historical Statistics of the United States: Colonial Times to 1970*, Bicentennial Edition, Part I, Washington D.C., 1975.
Note: No figures available for 1940. No figures available for England for 1950. Northern Ireland not included for 1930-70.

What I find even more interesting is that Italians are the ones who often laugh the hardest at Italian jokes. It expresses their rejection of Italianness and acceptance of the melting pot. Those who do not reject their Italianness stay outside the melting pot. Some remnants of Italian values, nonetheless, come through those who melt. Spaghetti is now American. So is pizza. The Italians also reinforce the place of Catholicism in American life.

A similar process occurred through Polish jokes. We lumped together all Slavic people (Russians, Czechs, Yugoslavians and so on) and called them Poles because the Poles were most visible, coming the fastest to the new world. This allowed us again to establish a place in society for such people which was negatively reinforced by jokes.

Mexicans have had the next most influence on the country as a whole, though in the Southwest their impact is far greater than some European groups. After World War 2 people from other Latin countries came in large numbers, especially from Cuba.

The last group, Asians, have been represented in the United States since the middle 1800s, notably by the Chinese who helped build the railroads of the West. California, of course, received most of these. But Asians never came in great numbers until recently. Also, the Chinese who did come tended to remain a closed community. Today the Vietnamese and other Indochinese refugees have high visibility.

Figure 5 is an attempt to visually represent the proportionate impact all these ethnic groups have had on the Middle-American value system. This is not a statistical chart of any kind but a weighted scale indicating who has affected the melting pot most and least based on the five factors I mentioned earlier: chronology, number, length of peak, shock and push/pull.

The circle represents all those in America. The areas

outside the circle are the host cultures from which the immigrants came. The shaded areas represent the proportion of those within each group who have not melted from their heritage. These ethnic holding grounds within geographic

**Figure 5**
**Model of American Dynamic Ethnicity Based on Value Impact**

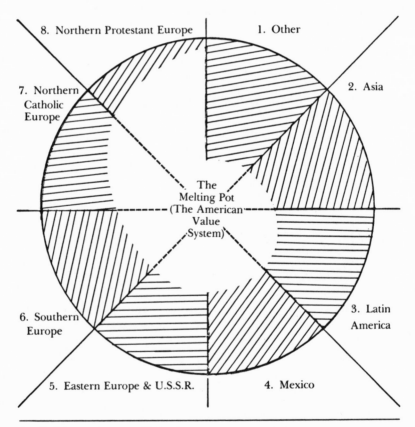

Key: O circle represents geographic America
/ / / / shaded area represents exoculture in America (immigrant holding grounds)
unshaded area represents the melting pot
1-8 areas beyond the circle represent host cultures from which immigrants came to the United States

America are often termed *exocultures*. The unshaded area in the circle represents those who have melted. Because the British and other Northern European Protestants dominate the melting pot, I have (arbitrarily) assigned them the number eight. The Northern European Catholics have contributed to the value system a little less, so they are seven, and so on.

## An Unbalanced Mixture

The melting pot is real; it is just not what we normally think it is. It is not an even mixture of all peoples and ideas. It is unbalanced, biased. Those who want to melt, will have to accept a culture dominated by Northern European Protestants. The further down the scale they are, the harder and longer it will be to melt.

An immigrant from England, for example, could, if he chose, lose his Englishness in about six months. Some may retain their distinctives as do those in the small British community that exists in New York City. But most will melt.

The Germans are another example.

In terms of size or the achievements of its members, the Germans ought certainly to be included among the principal ethnic groups of the city [of New York]. If never quite as numerous as the Irish, they were indisputably the second largest group in the late nineteenth century, accounting for perhaps a third of the population and enjoying the highest reputation. But today, while German influence is to be seen in virtually every aspect of the city's life, the Germans *as a group* are vanished. No appeals are made to the German vote, there are no German politicians in the sense that there are Irish or Italian politicians, there are in fact few Germans in political life and, generally speaking, no German component in the structure of the ethnic interests of the city.

The logical explanation of this development, in terms

of the presumed course of American social evolution, is simply that the Germans have been "assimilated" by the Anglo-Saxon center.[3]

In contrast, it takes almost three generations for many Chinese to enter the American middle class—if they ever do. Some families in San Francisco's Chinatown go back five or six generations, all within the Chinese community. It is far easier to move from Taiwan to Chinatown than from Chinatown to middle-class San Francisco. To put it another way, if a man from Chinatown marries an American, moves to Kansas, and they have a son who moves to Iowa, that son will have far less contact with Chinatown than Chinatown has with Taiwan.

The same is true in other communities, though less so. A Mexican can cross the border and enter the Mexican community in Los Angeles in a few hours. It may take years to cross the border into Middle America, perhaps two generations. During the revolution in Portugal in the mid-seventies, six thousand newspapers were flown daily from Lisbon to Newark. Why? Because the Portuguese community in Newark was far more interested in what was going on in Portugal than in New York. Their values drew their attention there. Ethnicity is another aspect of our urbanized culture that is a far greater barrier to cross than geography.

The system illustrated in Figure 5 also reinforces itself. The longer it takes to immigrate to the center of the pot, the more likely it is that an exoculture will develop as a means of mutual support and protection. The lower the number in Figure 5, the stronger the exoculture. The stronger the exoculture, the more difficult it is to step over the line into Middle America.

Glazer and Moynihan conclude their book *Beyond the Melting Pot* by indicating how ethnicity is woven together with the other lines of communication:

We have tried to show how deeply the pattern of ethnicity is impressed on the life of the city. Ethnicity is more than an influence on events; it is commonly the source of events. Social and political institutions do not merely respond to ethnic interests; a great number of institutions exist for the specific purpose of serving ethnic interests. This in turn tends to perpetuate them. In many ways, the atmosphere of New York City is hospitable to ethnic groupings: it recognizes them and rewards them, and to that extent encourages them.[4]

## The Nonvolunteer Immigrants

By this time the careful reader will have noticed that there are three major groups which are not represented at all in Figure 5. These are the three nonvolunteer immigrant groups. The three are not on the chart because they represent a zero or a negative factor in regard to the melting pot. Their values are essentially unmeltable. This negative factor is even expressed in the way we talk about them: the Indian problem, the Puerto Rican problem and the Black problem.

The first, the Indians (Native Americans) are not technically immigrants since they were already on the continent before the English arrived. But they were forced to become part of the United States; so I include them here. In the process of coercing them into the United States, we rejected Indian values. There is almost no Indian value that I can find that is a significant part of the mainstream American value system. We have adopted barbecuing, archery and other things, but we seldom credit these as being part of Indian culture. When Indians are visible, they are negative. If we have games of cowboys and Indians, the Indians always lose. The broken treaties and inhumane treatment of the Indians have been ignored in our history texts. Because the Indians still only number approximately one million, we have been able to keep that problem hidden and pretend that the Indians are not there.

The second nonvolunteer immigrant group is the Puerto Ricans. They are nonvolunteer in that the island came into the hands of the United States after the Spanish-American War of 1898. The people then became citizens of the United States. All other nations, once they began to come in too quickly, were put on a quota system. But we cannot stop the Puerto Ricans. They keep coming. Between 1950 and 1965 one-third of the population of Puerto Rico moved to the United States, half of whom live in the New York area. It just finally got to the point where we could not handle it anymore, and we began to ignore the Puerto Ricans. Irrational fear of Puerto Ricans developed because there was no control on how many could come in. They are citizens and can move as they please. To replace this kind of control another was substituted—Puerto Rican values became negative.

The third nonvolunteer group is the American Blacks. They are here because they were forced to come as slaves. In 1860 4.5 million slaves were freed. They were given citizenship, but they were not given land, jobs or training. They were not given any means by which they could be incorporated into the cultural value system. The result was that almost any Black value became negative. About a half million did manage to immigrate into the mainstream in the fifteen years following the Civil War. But soon the country could take no more and reconstruction ended. The history of Black Americans shows that about every twenty years the system opens up and absorbs several hundred thousand Blacks who give up their values and accept those of Middle America. Then the system again closes and won't allow any more in.

Absorption is a terribly hard process, because it is difficult to give up Blackness when one's skin remains the same color. But Blacks have wrestled with that for a hundred years. Some have worked through it successfully. Not all of these are Uncle Toms. Some have sold themselves to get into the system, but some have found creative ways to get in.

Some Blacks, of course, argue that it is pointless even to try to get into the mainstream. If you are going to be an American, you are going to have to reject your Blackness. This was the fight of the sixties, the attempt to get Blackness accepted as American. There are varying opinions of whether that was successful or not.

I am personally more concerned about the regression that has taken place in the last few years. Virtually all of the gains that took place in the years between 1959 and 1974 have been withdrawn. Just as in years past, after a period when Blacks have been accepted, the system cannot accept any more and it closes the Blacks off.

While perhaps half the Black population has achieved some degree of assimilation, the rest are again locked in the holding grounds of the rural sharecropper South and the urban ghettos. Those two holding grounds contain a population of over twelve million people whom the system ignores.

After the Vietnam War ended in 1975, a massive national effort was made to accommodate a quarter million Vietnamese refugees. Spurred on by a sense of moral responsibility and guilt, groups all over the country tried to find them jobs and housing. If it took a year to get them all out of Air Force camps and two years to find a permanent place for them in society when the country was so highly motivated, how long will it take to absorb twelve million Blacks the country does not want? But the extent of the problem is just not seen. To most, it does not exist.

I have conducted an informal survey with various groups. I hand out a piece of paper and ask people to account for all Black Americans by the occupation of the head of the house. Thus the figure for high professionals would not only include doctors, lawyers and the like but their families as well. The other categories range from medium and lower professionals to skilled and unskilled labor, unemployed and illegal professions. When the average White suburbanite totals these figures, the result is about three million Blacks. Rarely have I seen it higher than eight million. Actually, there are over twenty-five million Blacks in America. Thus, when Whites say we have a housing problem for Blacks, and the Blacks agree, the Whites are thinking, say, two hundred thousand and the Blacks are thinking two million.

Institutional racism is coming back into our culture, and it frightens me. I saw a simple manifestation of this just recently when I was in a Walden Bookstore. In one section I counted twenty-seven cheap paperbacks that dealt with the subject of Black-White slavery-sex relationships, all sort of interwoven and tied together. On the front cover was the old theme of a Black slave in the South being caught out in the woods with his mistress or of the White lady going down into the slave quarters or the Black male raping a White woman. These themes are part of a mythology that was developed in order to put across the idea that Black males are to be feared and controlled. If you give them a certain amount of freedom, we say, certain results will follow.

Where does this literature come from? From somebody who is clever enough to recognize that this is a theme that the American people want to believe again. So they capitalize. They package it in a slightly new format: pseudohistory of the South. And it sells because somebody wants to buy it. The end result is to reinforce all the myths that the sixties attempted to debunk. There was a whole body of literature written in the sixties that discredits those myths and shows that they were created for the purpose of destroying the Black male image. But it is ignored.

The July 1977 blackout in New York City is another indication of the turnaround that has occurred recently. Sociologists are still trying to understand why only Blacks and Puerto Ricans responded to the power failure by getting into the streets to take whatever they could get. Many consider it a simple issue of robbery. But if we understand the degree to which the American system rejects Blackness and Puerto Ricanness, we can understand the response of total disrespect for the system that cut them off.

A few years ago *Time* ran a brief article called "The Irregular Economy" which further illustrates how Blacks and Puerto Ricans are cut off from the system. It begins,

> For many have-not blacks, Puerto Ricans and other ghettoized minorities, the exemplar of business success is the jaunty dude in a wide-brimmed hat and high-heeled shoes who has made good—as a pimp. A few highly enterprising procurers pocket $100,000 a year. Indeed, crimes like narcotics peddling, prostitution and gambling are major moneymaking activities in the ghettos. They constitute a kind of irregular economy.... Though figures are imprecise, the turnover in the ghetto from narcotics, numbers, prostitution and other rackets amounts to at least $5 billion a year. According to one study, the black population of Brooklyn's Bedford-Stuyvesant section spent $88 million on drugs and policy gambling in 1970—about $11 million more than it collected in welfare.... The numbers operation alone had an annual payroll of $15 million, making it the biggest private employer in the area.... Some criminal entrepreneurs plow back a part of their earnings into legitimate ventures like dry-cleaning shops, real estate developments, bars, nonlicensed gypsy-cab fleets.... "There is community support for such crimes because it delivers vital services," says [Columbia University Professor Francis] Lanni.... Opinions differ on how Gov-

ernment should deal with the irregular economy. The Lasswell-McKenna report on Bedford-Stuyvesant calls for legalized gambling as a means of taking the play away from criminals. . . . Poor blacks tend to be against such a change because they distrust government, and they figure that the proceeds from gambling would be taken away from the black numbers runners and other local operatives.

The middle class gets uptight because they feel the government gives too many handouts. The poor distrust the government because they see where the handouts go. All the welfare money that comes into the city, by order of the government, must be used immediately. You cannot *buy* a house with it. You cannot *save* it in the bank. You cannot *invest* it in any way. You can pay as much as $400 per month in rent, but you will not be allowed to pick up a mortgage for $150 per month. Therefore, most of the money that comes from welfare goes into the hands of people in Bedford-Stuyvesant and Harlem and stays there for one cycle and then flips back out to Middle America. Welfare is a major route by which money is poured from government back into the suburbs, because that is where most of the landlords live. The poor have the money in their pocket for a week and then hand it on. Food stamps work the same way. The money comes in, it goes into a big grocery chain and in one hop it is back in suburban banks.

This is why *Time* says, "Poor blacks tend to be against [legalized gambling] because they distrust government, and they figure that the proceeds from gambling would be taken away from the black numbers runners and other local operatives." They want the gambling to stay in the hands of the Mafia and others who run it because the Mafia will reinvest that in legal businesses like taxi cabs, restaurants and dry-cleaning establishments. It is one of the main ways the ghetto gets any improvements. The *Time* article continues: "Lisle C. Carter, a Cornell University sociologist, notes that ghetto crime 'is a source of investment resources, of both equity and debt capital.' Some criminal kingpins, for example, lend money to people who want to go in honest business. Carter warns against moving too fast in rooting out crime in the ghetto lest this capital source dry up, leaving the inhabitants worse off than ever." *Time's* conclusion is a stark one. "Until more blacks are given greater economic opportunity, the brutalizing irregular economy may be the only crack at the free enterprise system."[5]

In Harlem about one-third of the population is on welfare. Another third—social workers, teachers, police officers and the like—is hired by the local and federal governments to supervise those on welfare. So well over half of Harlem is directly or indirectly controlled by the government which is itself, to a great extent, the handmaid of the suburban value system. The sixties did not change the negative perception we have of such people. They are a people to be controlled, not accommodated.

If this seems extreme, consider also that in 1978 over one-third of the people arrested in the United States were Black, but Blacks are only 11% of the total population of the country. In Maryland, for example, twelve Blacks are imprisoned for every White.[6]

Bill Pannell, director of a program for Black pastors at Fuller Seminary, says that in the long run "probably the greatest single threat to the black community is the white community's diminished commitment to a society under law. Law has become the province of vested interests. It is no longer informed by a relationship with religion. As a result, law has become the handmaid of order rather than justice. And order is defined by the ruling class, by people who can afford the best judges money can buy."[7]

Certainly most are in prison because they committed crimes, but the value system left them almost no alternative.

173

It has refused to accept Black values as positive.

## A Third Way

What alternative is there? The people of the ghetto are not going to go to the federal government. It has perpetuated the negative value the melting pot places on Blacks and Puerto Ricans. The alternative is for the church to establish a third system that provides people with the same kind of real help that the Mafia does. We, as Christians, if our commitment is to people, must understand what every kid in the ghetto understood long before Lisle C. Carter came down from Cornell University. If we can provide genuine economic relief, people will pour into the church. The Black Muslims (now called the American Muslim Mission) have demonstrated that. Our call to salvation must include more than salvation from sin. It must include salvation to Christian community that pays the rent, puts clothes on my back, and gives me people that I can fellowship with and trust. I'll join that. But just freedom from sin, that's meaningless. If the church can become a living, visible, demonstrative community in the city, we can start any kind of evangelism.

That is a very large *if*. We in the church must change our thinking before that *if* can come to pass. Let me highlight three issues we must consider seriously: first, how the lines of communication in ethnicity affect our Christian witness; second, how ethnicity affects our approach to missions; and third, how ethnicity affects our own value system.

First, the lines of communication. Rarely is the communication system of Middle America hooked up with that of ethnic exocultures. They run parallel and never intersect. In Philadelphia, for example, Dr. Lee, a pastor of a Korean church is an adjunct professor in a Bible school in the Korean community of Los Angeles and also in Seoul, Korea. You do not find him teaching the Word of God anywhere else in Philadelphia except in the Korean community. Yet he is a highly qualified man. In fact, churches five blocks away from his know less about what he is doing than churches in Los Angeles or in Seoul because his communication follows the lines of least resistance.

In Philadelphia two dozen churches meet and preach in the Korean language. And because of this they have no fellowship outside the Korean community. They are Korean Christians serving the Korean community. An interesting sidelight is that graduates of Westminster Theological Seminary went to Korea as missionaries fifty years ago to develop a church. Those churches are migrating back to Philadelphia; yet they lack communication with Westminster Seminary.

Because of cultural barriers, many do not know that there is a federation of over five hundred evangelical, Spanish-speaking churches in New York—and that does not cover all Spanish-speaking churches. There are also Puerto Rican churches in New York that send their young people back to Puerto Rico to study the Bible. Chinese churches as well often send their young people to Taiwan to study the Bible. A recent congress of the Chinese Christian community met in Hong Kong with some three thousand representatives. One of the main topics of discussion was the evangelization of the Chinese in North America. The Chinese communities in New York, Philadelphia, Chicago and San Francisco knew about that conference and its implications for them. Hardly any of the rest of us got the word. That kind of communication is important to the ongoing existence of the Chinese churches in America, but it is not on their agenda to communicate with other American churches.

A tremendous drive is necessary to get out of an urban ethnic community and to begin communicating to Middle America. Should we require ethnic churches to make all the

175

effort to come to us to communicate? I think not. There is cost to be paid on both sides if communication is to take place, but the cost for ethnic groups is greater than for those of us in Middle America. Their cost is possible rejection by their exoculture, their ethnic community, if they become too closely identified with White America. The lower the number as seen in Figure 5, the greater is the pull to stay in the exoculture and the greater the cost to those who communicate on our terms. Such an identification could destroy them or their ministry. The cost for us is giving up the notion that Christians have to look alike. It means acknowledging the validity of other cultures and the richness they have to offer our cultural form of Christianity.

Admittedly I am suggesting something foreign to our way of thinking. The flow is toward the center of the circle in Figure 5. We speak of integrating the Vietnamese or the Cubans or the Blacks *into* White society. We never speak of reversing the flow, of integrating into Black society. This one-way communication is the cause of great tensions in the nation.

The Black-White confrontation is like a twelve-volt resistor attached to a six-volt wire. By the time you get enough voltage to jump the resistor, the wire is burned out. Likewise, by the time Blacks lift their voices loud enough so they can be heard, there is a riot. Then we reject that form of communication, saying it is extreme.

It is up to us in the White community to go to them. We should not attempt to cross the cultural barrier to the non-Christian Black community. We should first go to the Christian Black community which is one step closer to our value system, though their Christian expression will still be different from what White Christians expect evangelicalism to look like. Then we should attempt to build a trust relationship with an individual in that Christian community.

After discovering through that person what God is already doing in that setting, you can ask, "How can my particular gifts be of service to you?" Then together you can walk into the non-Christian community with a bond of trust between you.

Of course this same principle holds between ethnic groups. Again, because the flow is toward the center, it is difficult to cross over from Korean to Puerto Rican or Italian to Chinese. Cultural diversity, as I argued in my cultural survey of the Bible in part one, is an essential element in Christianity because God wants to save all nations and because his nature is reflected in the diversity of peoples he has made. He also showed the legitimacy of entering into different cultures on their own terms through Joseph in Egypt, Daniel in Babylon and Barnabas in Antioch. Can we do any less?

## The Credible Missionary

The second major area urban ethnicity affects is our view of missions. As we have seen, the exocultures within America are in vigorous communication with their host cultures around the world. Africans are well informed of race relations in the United States. Therefore, more and more new missionaries are being asked on their arrival in Africa, "What do you think of the Black problem in America?" Africans are not as concerned with the missionaries' solutions as with how much they are aware of the problem and what their attitudes are toward the problem. Africans realize that their attitudes are a good barometer of what their attitudes will be toward the church in Africa. If missionaries can show a deep understanding and concern for the Black problem of America, their acceptance with the church of Africa is going to be much more rapid and smooth.

I remember one day being in the company of three missionaries when an African asked, "What are the trees of

America like?" Almost simultaneously, the three missionaries began to speak. One missionary said, "When you
stand on a hill and look out over the vast rolling tops of dark
evergreens, it's a thrilling picture to see trees as far as the
eye can see." Another was saying in the meantime, "Why, in
America we hardly have any trees at all." A third was saying, "The trees in America are as big around as twelve
men's arms can reach and stand more than one hundred
feet tall." You see, the one had come from the evergreen
forest of Maine, another had come from the deserts of
Arizona and the third from the redwood forest of California. Each was speaking about America, but each was
speaking about the America that he knew, and none was
truly representing the picture of America. Let us realize
that virtually every missionary is speaking of a White,
middle-class, Protestant America and not of America as the
home of twenty-five million Blacks. What does this mean to
the Black people of Africa? It means our statement of
concern for Black Africa is a sham when we have not shown
concern for Black America.

One solution would be for every foreign mission agency
to link up with an established urban ministry in the United
States paralleling the area of its overseas concerns. This
would be used both as a training ground for missionary
candidates and as a learning ground for the agency as a
whole for what the overseas operation should be like.

Apart from that rather ideal solution, individuals considering missions in, say Peru, should first involve themselves with an indigenous Spanish-speaking ministry or
church here at home. The experience would be invaluable.

Another possibility would be for agencies to seek more
Black candidates to work in Africa, more Hispanics to work
in Latin America and more Chinese to work in Singapore.
First, their background often gives them a rapport overseas
that may take years for a White to develop. They would also

help broaden the agency's own horizons culturally.

Second, hiring American ethnics aids credibility. Black candidates in our missions would help the witness of a White mission in African countries. The American Embassy in Nairobi has deliberately gone out of its way to make almost one-third of its staff Black Americans. Under the Carter administration, the U.S. ambassador to the U.N. (dominated by Third-World countries) was Black. These steps are political, but they are appreciated by the governments of Africa, and I think that missions would do well to learn from our government's example.

Third, ethnic missionaries, especially if they are mature, could become a third force in church-mission communications. Because of their color they can affiliate closer with the church than White missionaries can. Yet, because they are Americans and have been exposed to the American culture, they would have some understanding of the White missionary. The White missionary could speak more freely to the Black missionary, and the African church member could more freely speak to the Black American missionary.

In pursuing this last possibility, however, we must be careful not to pull the rug out from under indigenous Black ministries in the United States by "stealing" their best people. Some Blacks, we pray, will feel called, however, to pursue such a ministry. Let us welcome them openly.

**The Failure of Rural Christianity**
Lastly, ethnicity—and the entire wave of urbanization flooding our world—affects our own value system. In this chapter I have highlighted the priority we have put on conformity to a culture dominated by Northern European Protestantism. While some melting has indeed occurred, my conclusion is the same as that of Glazer and Moynihan.

The point about the melting pot is that it did not happen.
. . . We may argue whether it was "nature" that returned

179

to frustrate continually the imminent creation of a single American nationality. The fact is that in every generation, throughout the history of the American republic, the merging of the varying streams of population differentiated from one another by origin, religion, outlook has seemed to lie just ahead—a generation, perhaps, in the future.... It is striking that in 1963, almost forty years after mass immigration from Europe to this country ended, the ethnic pattern is still so strong in New York City.[8]

This is still true nearly twenty years after Glazer and Moynihan's study. This failure to be "One Nation under God" should alone cause us to ask if we should continue to embrace this dream. The added failure of the church to substantially Christianize the city would seem to make the view even more untenable. We have assumed that if everyone would accept Middle-American values, we could all be "One Nation under God." This has not happened and the failure is most visible in the city.

Consider who is in the city: Asians, Latinos, Mexicans, Slavs, Italians. These are either non-Christian or Catholic cultures. And even much of the Catholicism in the city is laced with overt or more subtle forms of superstition. In such a setting the mayor of Newark can be re-elected while sitting in prison, and no one blinks. In rural-minded America, however, one small misstep by a president and the country is bellowing for his resignation. Why the double standard? Because Northern European Protestantism dominates the culture as a whole. But it has not touched the city.

Such a failure in the city is magnified if the wave to come is urbanization. To be effective in such a world, the church must throw off its cultural blinders. We must ask ourselves, "Are we committed first to the melting pot or to Christ?" If we are committed to the former, our attitude will be, "The city is a hopeless pit. There is nothing we can do for it. Let us use our gifts where we will see fruit." If we are committed first to Christ, our attitude will be, "Our values have failed in the city. Because we are committed to reach it for Christ's sake, let us let go of these values and adopt new ones that will fulfill the Great Commission." I am not suggesting that the "new values" merely be what works to get the job done. Rather I am suggesting we go back to the Bible to see what values transcend all cultures and can therefore be applied to any culture. This is the thrust of the next two chapters.

I still remember the day I was in a stadium of fifty thousand Africans watching a soccer match. The game was lousy. No one was excited about it. So at half time some politician decided he was going to say a few words to an apathetic crowd. But he could not rouse them either. Therefore he got onto his favorite subject—nasty White people, the bad colonialists, the awful English and what should have been done to them when they were in power. I think I was the only White in the whole stadium.

Finally, he got them going enough that they were ready to lynch somebody. I was about eighteen rows from the exit. Some very angry faces began turning and recognizing that I was there. It was an uncomfortable moment. A mob was about to develop.

I was with ten members of the church, some young people and some couples. But they turned to the crowd with the focus of their eyes on the people closest to them and just said, "He's with us." To the twenty or thirty people sitting nearby, that meant nothing would happen so that section quieted down. You could then see the quiet move through the crowd like wind across a wheat field. As each group realized that nothing was going to happen, they lost interest and turned away.

We are different, but we can still be one. Indeed, despite

the real differences that exist, we in the church can be a source of protection for each other and a source of peace to the world.

# Part 3
## Christ beyond Culture

# 11
# One in Christ
# in Truth
# and Love

I CAN STILL REMEMBER when I first tried to communicate the gospel to a Maasai tribesman sitting under a tree in his red blanket. He had never been more than a few miles from his home. But I could see in my conversation with him that he valued three things: that he could walk fifty miles a day; that he knew all that there was to know about his cows; that that he was a Maasai, the most important people on the earth. He could see that I was not a Maasai, that I did not know a thing about cows and that I could hardly walk ten miles. So to him I was completely valueless. He had an air of superiority that began to get to me. I asked myself, "How can I communicate my very important message when he can't care less about anything I have to offer?"

As a result I gave up talking about Jesus Christ and started talking about my travels, my education and my car. Of course we were not communicating, but I persisted. In fact, I decided to try to sell him my Volkswagen. It started as a joke, but it became quite serious. In the bartering process one can always back out, but I found that with all my bartering and pushing I could not get him to trade one of his cows (which I could have bought on the open market for about $15) for my Volkswagen (which was worth $3000 in Nairobi at that moment). Cows were the important things in his life, and anybody who did not know everything about cows was, in his view, an idiot. I knew nothing about cows; therefore, I was an idiot. Then how could I convince him to listen to me about Christianity?

I tried to convince him that I knew something about cars and that I knew something about philosophy and Plato. But that meant about as much to him as the man in the moon, who he hadn't heard of either. I began to realize that we had to have some common values before we could begin to communicate.

This is true whenever two people encounter each other. Recall Beth, who was mentioned in chapter two. She was living with a man because she needed protection. I had to examine how I viewed her and the decisions she was making. Likewise, as I work on college campuses I need to reconsider the Greek system of logic that has so influenced Western Christianity. Or if I am looking for a church, I need to ask myself whether the vibrant preaching of a Black pastor ought to become a part of my worship. As I come into contact with different cultures, different sets of priorities, even different expressions of values similar to mine, I need a biblical value system by which to judge them all. Truth and love, I believe, are at the core of this system.

## Who Is God?

John Perkins in *A Quiet Revolution* writes, "If you take all the verses in the Bible and organize them under themes, the two major themes with the most individual verses supporting them are God's hate for idolatry and God's concern for the poor and the oppressed."[1] You could also turn those two themes into positive statements. God's concern is truth, and God's concern is love.

These themes are prominent from Genesis through Revelation. There are dozens of places in the Bible in which those two themes are even put into one verse.[2]

When Abraham, for example, sent his servant to look for a wife for Isaac, the servant introduced himself to Rebekah by saying, "Blessed be the LORD God of my master Abraham, who hath not left destitute my master of his mercy and his truth" (Gen. 24:27 KJV). In other words, he identified himself as a servant of Abraham who followed the God of mercy and truth. God was just beginning to introduce himself to Abraham, but these two themes were already impressed on him.

Later, when Jacob was on the verge of his confrontation with Esau and in need of God's help, he prayed, "I am not worthy of the least of all the mercies, and of all the truth, which thou hast shewed unto thy servant" (Gen. 32:10 KJV). On Mount Sinai after Moses requested to see God's glory, his essence, "the LORD passed by before him, and proclaimed, The LORD, the LORD God, merciful and gracious, longsuffering and abundant in goodness and truth" (Ex. 34:6 KJV). These two characteristics are at the core of God's being.

Proverbs says, "Do not let kindness and truth leave you; bind them around your neck, write them on the tablet of your heart" (Prov. 3:3 NASB). Remind yourself of them, memorize them, know them; because if you have mercy and truth, then you have direction for your life. The prophets tell us the same. "He has told you, O man, what is good; and what does the LORD require of you but to do justice, to love kindness, and to walk humbly with your God?" (Mic. 6:8 NASB). Justice and judgment, executing God's law, comes under the heading of truth. Kindness and mercy are forms of his love. Micah is not alone. Hosea (2:19; 12:6) and Zechariah (8:19) proclaim the same theme.

In the New Testament Christ condemns the Pharisees for ignoring what is truly important. "Woe to you, scribes and Pharisees, hypocrites! for you tithe mint and dill and cummin, and have neglected the weightier matters of the law, justice and mercy and faith" (Mt. 23:23). John introduces Christ by twice highlighting these as the center of Christ's person and work. "The Word became flesh and dwelt among us, full of grace and truth. . . . Grace and truth came through Jesus Christ" (Jn. 1:14, 17). Two other New Testament writers pick up the theme as well—Paul in Ephesians 4:15 and Peter in 1 Peter 1:22.

### The Reluctant Missionary

The problem we have with these two themes is our tendency to absolutize them, to turn them into abstract principles rather than living realities. When we do this, of course, we are likely to polarize the two or to emphasize one over the other. "Love is all that matters. We must be sure all our thoughts and actions are in love." This thinking creates license. Others might say, "But if truth is not preeminent, how can you say you even know love is important? Truth must come first." This thinking creates legalism.

Jonah offers us an example. This reluctant missionary refused God's call to go preach judgment to Nineveh, the capital of Israel's enemy, Assyria. Why? Not because he was afraid of persecution but, in his own words, because "I knew that thou art a gracious God and merciful, slow to anger, and abounding in steadfast love, and repentest of evil" (Jon. 4:2). In his head he knew God was both truth (he was to preach judgment) and love (God would forgive Ninevah). But Jonah had failed to integrate these in his own life. He wanted Israel's enemy destroyed. He did not want to give them a chance to repent.

His understanding was so limited, in fact, that God had to show him his judgment and mercy twice—once by putting him in the belly of the great fish and then getting him out; then by comparing Jonah's concern for a plant and God's concern for Ninevah.

Opposing or separating truth and love represents a false dichotomy because both truth and love come from God, who is a unity. It is in God as a unified *person* that they are joined.

We too often assume that if we have a comprehensive and consistent collection of propositions about God that we will then have a clear concept of God. This is not so because God is a person who will not be reduced to mere propositions. We must also know him in his actions and in our experience. This is a very Hebrew notion. To be real, truth must be more than an idea; it must also be action consistent with that belief. In God's personality, truth and love are consistently expressed to us. In him we have both and so avoid both legalism and license.

Yet God is infinite. How can we who are finite adequately express truth and love in full unity?" some may respond. We are able to express them because we too are persons. Admittedly, we cannot do so as fully as God. God is unchanging and we are changing. Yet, we by his Spirit, are moving toward God, becoming like him.

## The Confessing King

David saw this process clearly in Psalm 5. "For thou art not a God who delights in wickedness; evil may not sojourn with thee. The boastful may not stand before thy eyes; thou hatest all evildoers. Thou destroyest those who speak lies; the LORD abhors bloodthirsty and deceitful men" (Ps. 5:4-6). How we agree with David! That's exactly what God is like, we say. But think a minute.

This is the David who on several occasions recognized

189

that he was wicked. "Evil may not sojourn with thee." David knew his own proud nature. "The boastful may not stand before thy eyes." David realized he had made some terrible mistakes in how he brought up Absalom. David was also so bloodthirsty that God would not allow him to build the Temple. "The LORD abhors bloodthirsty and deceitful men." David is not talking about some abstract person in Psalm 5. He is saying, "God, you will not tolerate any of these things—and I am all of these things!"

Yet in the next verse he says, "But I through the abundance of thy steadfast love will enter thy house." David says in essence, "God, I know you are absolute truth into whose presence I cannot come, but I also know that because you are absolute love, I can enter in."

In verse 8 David then says, "Lead me, O LORD, in thy righteousness." David shifts from God's absoluteness to his own finiteness and imperfection, and anticipates the fuller truth and love God is going to put in him. As we approach other value systems, other cultures, we must come humbly recognizing our own limitations and faults. We must see that God cannot have us in his presence but that he is also changing us into his likeness. This can also prevent arrogance on our part because God is working the same process in other cultures.

Like Jonah, we condemn the city because it is our enemy. Our pride blinds us to the fact that people in the city also have partial truth and love which God is making more complete. Indeed, by learning about other cultures, we can then learn about the truth and love God has given them which we do not yet possess. The result? The whole church is strengthened as its view of God becomes more complete. This is one of the great benefits of missions. But if we absolutize our culture and box God inside it, we will not be enriched. Rather we will die—if God does not cut us off first.

The isolationist, provincial mindset has captured much of the missionary thinking of the church. "You go over there and do missions, and we'll stay here and take care of our own little secure selves. But don't let what is happening over there affect us." I ran into this when under the African Inland Mission I helped bring the mission field within thirty miles of some of our supporting churches. Some could not handle it. That mission field was too close, and they did not like it. They would not support it. Much of the money that we got to operate the ministry in Newark came from outside of New York and New Jersey. People from Los Angeles were glad to support our urban ministry in Newark. (But make sure you do not ask them to get involved in Los Angeles!)

## Light and Love: 1 John
I began to work out the interrelationship of truth and love through a study of the first letter of John. I will highlight some of my findings, but it is certainly worth thorough study by anyone who wants to understand how God's absoluteness is lived out in our finiteness.

After a brief introduction, John begins with God's absoluteness, "God is light" (1 Jn. 1:5). The next two verses say we must not only believe that but live it as well. How is that possible if we are finite? "The blood of Jesus his Son cleanses us from all sin" (1:7). God's love makes it possible for us to walk in truth. The result is fellowship (1:7), harmony and unity among God's people.

But if we are arrogant enough to claim that we have all truth, that there is no darkness in us, "if we say we have no sin, we deceive ourselves, and the truth is not in us" (1:8). Indeed, the very act of admitting our falsehood is the necessary prerequisite for receiving truth. "If we confess our sins, he is faithful and just, and will forgive our sins and cleanse us from all unrighteousness" (1:9). God is not expecting us to be absolute truth; he is absolute truth. But God does expect all of us to live up to the truth that he has revealed to us.

This applies directly to what you have been reading in this book. You may have begun to hear some things that burden you. You may be beginning to say, "I am responsible for so many things." But God does not expect us to be instant crosscultural experts. He does, however, want us to begin changing. So ask yourself, "How much of this, Lord, do you want me to apply this month?" And then begin to do it. Begin to activate the truth God has given you. God is not expecting us to love all the people of the world. But he is expecting us to love those people with whom he has brought us in contact.

By living consistently with what we know to be true, we confirm that we know the one God. "By this we may be sure that we know him, if we keep his commandments" (2:3). Not only this, "But whoever keeps his [God's] word, in him truly love for God is perfected" (2:5). This equation of truth and love is repeated in 2:8-10.

While the last half of chapter 2 goes on to emphasize the theme of truth, John rolls back in chapter 3 to the theme of love. Chapter 4 focuses on truth and 5 deals primarily with love. Thus the book's structure, with its intertwining of the two themes, reinforces their essential unity. I want to point out only a few more specific verses.

"See what love the Father has given us, that we should be called children of God; and so we are. The reason why the world does not know us is that it did not know him" (3:1). In the world, people are all tied up in themselves, creating their own gods. They do not understand us because their attention is focused on themselves rather than on God. Even so, "it does not yet appear what we shall be, but we know that when he appears we shall be like him, for we shall see him as he is. And every one who thus hopes in him purifies himself as he is pure" (3:2). Our present truth and love is being transformed. We are in the process of moving toward God.

"This is the message which you have heard from the beginning, that we should love one another, and not be like Cain who was of the evil one and murdered his brother. And why did he murder him? Because his own deeds were evil and his brother's righteous. Do not wonder, brethren, that the world hates you" (3:11-13). We are back in Genesis, contrasting the line of Seth and the line of Cain. So we marvel not that the line of Cain hates us when we show God's love to one another.

For many years we thought of our country as a Christian nation. The church had control over large sections of society. Hospitals are still named St. Mary's, St. Luke's and the like because they were under the control of the church. A hundred years ago most of our private universities were church institutions.

But the church is no longer in control of such enterprises. So we should seriously question whether we are manifesting God's love by simply, for instance, donating funds to a public tutoring program. Such involvement is not wrong if we are doing so as a fellowship of people who love God, one another and the world. But I question if we are manifesting God's love by volunteering as an individual to teach in a secular tutoring program. How does that differ from what non-Christians are doing? If, however, we undertake such a project as part of the body of Christ we can show God's love to the world. In this way, God's truth is clearly revealed. Our love for each other, which the world cannot reproduce, carries truth to the world.

This is what John Perkins's wholistic ministry, Voice of Calvary, is doing in Mississippi. As they begin to help people develop economically, as they confront the establishment with justice, they are leading people toward truth.

They can begin to sense when people are ready to accept the gospel. Of course some individuals have a special gift of evangelism. But we all need to become more involved in the broader process of communicating truth corporately to the world. After a person comes to a personal confrontation with truth, he or she will still continue to move toward truth. Only once they come to know Christ we call it discipleship.

When the body of Christ as a body is strong, then it can begin to redeem a culture as a whole. Individually, the truth God gives us is finite. It is finite collectively, too, but far less so. And if a group of Christians in one culture can begin showing love to a group of Christians in another culture, the truth is magnified and the world is changed.

"What about doctrinal differences? We cannot fellowship with people whose ideas are semipagan." John has an answer for that too. "Beloved, do not believe every spirit, but test the spirits to see whether they are of God; for many false prophets have gone out into the world. By this you know the Spirit of God: every spirit which confesses that Jesus Christ has come in the flesh is of God, and every spirit which does not confess Jesus is not of God" (4:1-3).

That is an awfully broad statement. Are you going to accept anyone who says that Jesus Christ is come in the flesh? In my experience, this has actually proven to be an adequate division line. If someone believes and lives in light of the fact that Jesus Christ is Lord and also man, that Jesus Christ is God but he came in the flesh to provide a way back to God, then that person has a fairly good grasp of what Christ and Christianity is all about. Some of the implications of these statements for our lives are taken up in the next chapter.

Beyond believing Jesus is human and Lord, of course, there can be some tremendous differences. But Christianity is Christ. Our unity is in him and in nothing else. "We know that the Son of God has come and has given us understanding, to know him who is true; and we are in him who is true, in his Son Jesus Christ. This is the true God and eternal life" (5:20).

# 12
## True
## Discipleship

A FEW YEARS AGO A LEADER of a Christian organization told me about a plan he was developing to evangelize the world by computer. It was a rather detailed and well-thought-out plan. People would ask the computer questions, and answers would flash on the screen. Of course, thanks to the computer, the answers would come in a tremendous variety, almost seeming to be personal. But they would be standard answers from the Word of God whose intent was to remove the problems these people faced so they could receive Christ. This would then be followed by a three-step plan of salvation. For example, after all the response cards from an evangelistic meeting had been collected, they could be put into the computer and answers would be ready before anyone left the meeting. Then people could accept Christ in a small side room that had computers available for them to use.

Today we find impersonal, group-imposed standards in

every aspect of our culture. The Western world is pitted against true discipleship. Because a large percentage of our population has reached a high standard of living through a rather sophisticated technology, individual standards have had to be eliminated and replaced with group standards.

For example, morally, some acts are not considered wrong, but getting caught is. Many people are a little dishonest with their income tax. Few actually stay within the speed limit. And a man thinks, if she's willing—why not? In other words, if everybody else does it, I can do it.

Success too is measured by group standards. Much of our lives is aimed at trying to find out what the present "in" standard is. Since this can be frustrating if it is up to the individual to find out what the group wants, we begin to develop institutions to reinforce our successes. We have programmed education; we have mass media.

The Urbana Student Missions Conventions are massive undertakings. I understand the need for efficient operation or nothing would happen. But I found it quite revealing (and a little humorous) to be in line with thousands of others, an amoebic blob waiting to register. Everything was running smoothly and steadily until I was foolish enough at one point to say, "I am different." Immediately the computer rejected me, and I was pushed out of the line into a small room with a closed door. It was some hours before my problem could be sorted out. Because I was an individual, I was a problem. This is the society that we live in.

The church has also fallen into the grip of society. We too have impersonal, group-imposed standards. If my church has three hundred people, and all the churches in my conference or district or neighborhood have two hundred, then I am successful. If all the youth groups in my area have twenty young people, and my group has twenty-five, I am successful. If all the evangelism teams are converting one person a month and my team is converting three, I am successful. If all the churches in my area are giving $2,000 a year to missions, and we are giving $3,000 a year to missions, we are successful. We measure success by growth. We have established standards and percentages for what we consider growth.

To achieve this end, we have institutionalized the church. To educate our youth we have established the Sunday school. To create fellowship for our youth we have established youth clubs. We have institutionalized prayer to Wednesday night, and worship to Sunday morning. And we have determined who is a good Christian and who is not by group standards. Anybody can look into the church and tell whether or not that sixteen-year-old boy is a good Christian or not. Does he attend youth fellowship? Does he bring a Bible to church? Does he please the elders of the congregation by not rocking the boat?

### "Who Do You Say That I Am?"

One of my purposes in this book has been to enlarge your vision of who Jesus is. This is important because if we are to follow Jesus (one of the most basic definitions of discipleship), we must know who he is. Luke 9 gives us this chance to step back from urbanization and ethnicity and culture to put our discussions in a larger setting. The person of Christ, then, can give us proper direction in contrast to the artificial standards often imposed on us.

Luke has arranged his material following the same principles John followed in chapter 4 of his Gospel. History is important and so facts are not changed. Rather, they are arranged differently on different occasions to teach larger lessons. In this way people are taught both history and important truths for their lives.

In chapter 9, Luke is about at the midpoint of Jesus' ministry. So he brings together some episodes to help his readers start drawing conclusions about who Jesus is.

The chapter begins with Jesus giving the Twelve a task. "And he called the twelve together and gave them power and authority over all demons and to cure diseases, and he sent them out to preach the kingdom of God and to heal" (vv. 1-2). After giving a few more instructions, it says, "Now Herod the tetrarch heard of all that was done, and he was perplexed, because it was said by some that John had been raised from the dead, by some that Elijah had appeared, and by others that one of the old prophets had risen. Herod said, 'John I beheaded; but who is this about whom I hear such things?' And he sought to see him" (vv. 7-9). This is followed in verse 10 by, "On their return the apostles told him what they had done."

It is a bit odd that Luke would drop this interlude about Herod right in the middle of the story of the disciples being sent out and then coming back. I believe Luke is using the words of Herod to raise a question: Who is this Jesus? Because of the context, however, it is not an academic question to be answered in a void. Rather it becomes a question of how Jesus' identity affects discipleship. Who Jesus is, implies Luke, should alter the way we follow him, the way we carry out the tasks he has given us to do. And especially if we are to be his witnesses, we better know who he is.

Once the apostles return, Jesus takes them apart to Bethsaida (v. 10). But the crowd follows and gathers, and Jesus becomes so absorbed with the crowd that he teaches them all day (v. 11). "Now the day began to wear away; and the twelve came to him and said to him, 'Send the crowd away, to go into the villages and country round about, to lodge and get provisions; for we are here in a lonely place'" (v. 12). But their concern for the crowd is really an excuse to get rid of them. They had come to tell Jesus all that they had done, and they had not yet had a chance. Jesus, sensing their spirit, turns to them and says, 'You give them some-

thing to eat.' They said, 'We have no more than five loaves
and two fish'" (v. 13). So Jesus fed the multitude. This is
Jesus' way of saying that the disciples are not really ready to
do his work because they do not know who he is. He is a person concerned with people and the needs of people. The
disciples were mostly concerned with reporting on their accomplishments, their successes.

The question is again raised in the following verses.
"Now it happened that as he was praying alone the disciples
were with him; and he said to them, 'Who do the people say
that I am?' And they answered, 'John the Baptist; but others
say, Elijah; and others, that one of the old prophets has
risen' " (vv. 18-19). These are the same possibilities Herod
worked with. All the answers are biblical yet they are all
wrong. So Jesus asked, " 'But who do you say that I am?'
And Peter answered, 'The Christ of God.' " Peter began to
perceive who Jesus really was, but his understanding was
not complete as later events showed. He had trouble living
out the implications of Jesus' identity.

What are these implications? There are implications first
for Jesus himself and then for those who would follow him.

"The Son of man must suffer many things, and be rejected by the elders and chief priests and scribes, and be
killed and on the third day be raised." And he said to all,
"If any man would come after me, let him deny himself
and take up his cross daily and follow me. For whoever
would save his life will lose it; and whoever loses his life
for my sake, he will save it. For what does it profit a man
if he gains the whole world and loses or forfeits himself?
For whoever is ashamed of me and of my words, of him
will the Son of man be ashamed when he comes in his
glory and the glory of the Father and of the holy angels.
But I tell you truly, there are some standing here who will
not taste death before they see the kingdom of God." (vv.
22-27)

This is one of the strongest statements in Scripture on what it means to follow Jesus. But it is in the context of needing to know who Jesus is before you can follow him.

The next paragraph picks up this theme too. "Now about eight days after these sayings he took with him Peter and John and James, and went up on the mountain to pray. And as he was praying, the appearance of his countenance was altered, and his raiment became dazzling white. And behold, two men talked with him, Moses and Elijah, who appeared in glory and spoke of his departure" (vv. 28-31). Who do the people say he is? Some say he is Moses; some say he is Elijah. The transfiguration makes it explicit that this is not who Jesus is.

"And a voice came out of the cloud, saying, 'This is my Son, my Chosen; listen to him!' " (v. 35). Who Jesus is, on the other hand, is also made explicit. Jesus is the Son of God. The progression has been who the people say Jesus is, who the disciples say he is, who Jesus says he is and finally who the Father himself says Jesus is. Intertwined with this is also the theme of what it means to follow such a person.

On the next day, they came down the mountain and were met by a man whose son had a demon. He tells Jesus, "And I begged your disciples [who were not on the mountain with you] to cast it out, but they could not" (v. 40). This is in stark contrast to verse 1, "He called the twelve together and gave them power and authority over all demons." Though Peter had said Jesus is Christ, and he and James and John went with Jesus to the top of the mountain, there were still the other disciples whose understanding was not as developed. They could not use the power that Jesus had already given them. Jesus' response is, "O faithless and perverse generation, how long am I to be with you and bear with you?" (v. 41). Jesus can give you all the power in the world, but if you don't know who he is, you cannot use it.

So once again Luke lifts up the question, " 'Let these words sink into your ears; for the Son of man is to be delivered into the hands of men.' But they did not understand this saying, and it was concealed from them, that they should not perceive it" (vv. 44-45). Despite Jesus' attempts to drag them along, to see him in a larger context, they still did not fully know who Jesus was. We too, as I hope this book has been encouraging us to do, must be asking ourselves whether or not we have the large vision of Jesus he wants us to have. In the last chapter I spoke of a value system that causes us to follow the light that God has put in front of us, that calls us to be faithful to that which he is revealing to us. As we obey that call, God then gives us more light to follow. More truth. More love. In so doing he expands our understanding of himself and of the world around us.

**Beyond Possibility**
As we saw with Peter in Acts 10—11, our culture tends to define possibility and impossibility for us.

Jesus also likes to take us out to the ends of our culture and say, "That's what you believe is possible? Let me show you what is really possible." And he leads us into the realm of the seemingly impossible—and that is faith. He takes us across the boundary of what our culture says cannot be done and does it. Jesus is not bound by our culture, he is beyond it. If we accept our culture's definition of who Jesus is, we do not know who he is. He is much larger than that. Because none of us know what our culture is doing to us, we have an obligation to find out.

A friend of mine, Dave, who graduated from Rutgers engineering school several years ago, has been working for a large corporation. The first month there somebody asked him to go out and buy coffee for the whole crew.

"Who's going to pay for it?" he asked.

"Just put in an expense form for mileage to cover the cost."

"I can't do that. That's not what it's for."

"Well, you had better do it," came the answer.

He was firm, however, so they got somebody else to do it.

Dave never got a promotion for the rest of that summer even though all the others did. Of course he noticed this and began asking about it. He discovered that this firm wanted people at the top who had submitted themselves to a system, people who had become corrupted and were therefore corruptible, people who the company could control in this way. Unless you were willing to do what you were told, there was no promotion. The main criterion for moving up was to so identify yourself with the system that by the time you got ready for management, you would have been so bought out by that system (you would already have done so many deceitful things) that you could no longer expose what they were doing in the home offices. Great corruption from tiny misdeeds grows.

Dave, however, stuck it out, working honestly within the system that tried to mold him. He did get a choice promotion eventually—to a position in which the company had to have someone who was scrupulously honest!

Our culture tries to mold us in other ways. One friend of mine is making $20,000 a year and is hurting because the recession cut back on his ability to make money through investment. Because he anticipated that extra income beyond his $20,000 salary, he is not able to keep up with the standard of living to which he has become adjusted. So at $20,000 a year, he is finding himself to be poor. Poverty, however, is relative. Poverty is defined for us by our culture. But society should not dictate the standard of living for Christians. Only God's Word should do that.

Every day we are being bombarded by mass media which define for us what is possible and impossible. Our family came home from the mission field with three children. We were making $7,500 a year. The first year we were home I put $1,400 in savings because we did not have any need for it. We had brought our African standard of living with us. The second year we put $200 in savings. The third year we could not pay the bills at the end of the month. Our culture had molded us into its own image. With ten years of living in a poverty culture, we suddenly found that even our Christian friends were putting pressure on us to get a better car, to have a TV, to enjoy this or that. We were being caught in a trap. So we began to cut some of these nonessentials that people will tell you are essential ("Oh, I couldn't *possibly* live without that!") and free up our money for God's glory.

It is not too early to confront the limits of your culture even while in college. Those on residential campuses could approach the school administration with a proposal to spend your third year of study in an urban context. Some administrators will look at this like going overseas for a year of study. They could easily make the arrangements with another institution to transfer credits. This could give you in your final year a new awareness of what the world around you is like and begin to give you an education that is more representative of the world as a whole.

## Six Signposts of Discipleship

While it is essential to know who Jesus is before we can follow him, Jesus is willing to allow us to follow him at any level of understanding. He then wants to bring us into a larger vision of him. At the end of Luke 9 we find six signposts on the road of discipleship.

"And an argument arose among them as to which of them was the greatest. But when Jesus perceived the thought of their hearts, he took a child and put him by his side, and said to them, 'Whoever receives this child in my name receives me, and whoever receives me receives him who sent me; for he who is least among you all is the one who is great' " (vv. 46-48). The disciples were arguing about who was the greatest, and Jesus says that is not leadership, that is not discipleship, that is not the kind of people he wanted following him. The first signpost is childlike humility, openness, curiosity and enthusiasm—not worldly jockeying for power and status.

Second, "John answered, 'Master, we saw a man casting out demons in your name, and we forbade him, because he does not follow with us.' But Jesus said to him, 'Do not forbid him; for he that is not against you is for you' " (vv. 49-50). How many times have we sought to condemn other Christians because they were not using our methods! But those who follow Jesus are not to be concerned with who else is following Jesus. We have no right to condemn, to cut down, to criticize or to negatively question the work of others just because they are different, just to build ourselves up. It can be legitimate to give critique as part of the body, to build one another up. But true discipleship has only one enemy.

The third signpost of discipleship emphasizes much of what has already been said in this book. "When the days drew near for him to be received up, he set his face to go to Jerusalem. And he sent messengers ahead of him, who went and entered a village of the Samaritans, to make ready for him; but the people would not receive him, because his face was set toward Jerusalem. And when his disciples James and John saw it, they said, 'Lord, do you want us to bid fire come down from heaven and consume them?' But he turned and rebuked them. And they went on to another village" (vv. 51-56). As we saw in John 4, Jews and Samaritans were antagonistic toward each other. Samaritans even harrassed pilgrims on the road to Jerusalem. The disciples responded in kind. But Jesus' plan went far beyond those cultural boundaries. Jesus saw that the disciples still had a heart full of racism. They wanted to destroy and burn out the Samaritans in revenge for a discourtesy. Jesus rebuked them, saying, "Let's simply go to another village."

How patient we are in explaining the gospel over and over to a friend or relative. But we preach the gospel once in the city, are rebuked by some angry young Black person who has all kinds of reasons to reject us, and we immediately pack up and leave because, "These people don't want to hear the gospel." Whole ministries have been torn out of a city because of a lack of commitment. Every summer people come into cities, pass out tracts and then scatter. We fear the city. We fear Blackness, ethnicity, the ghetto. The disciples had the same ignorance and fear. Fear that turns to rejection is not the kind of discipleship that Jesus has in mind.

Discipleship is not seeking worldly status; it is not cutting down other Christians; it is not racism. Luke gives three more signposts in the last six verses of chapter 9 which emphasize the priority of discipleship. "As they were going along the road, a young man said, 'I will follow you wherever you go.' And Jesus said to him, 'Foxes have holes, and birds of the air have nests; but the Son of man has nowhere to lay his head' " (vv. 57-58). If we are going to follow Jesus, we are not going to have any fringe benefits. They may come our way, but they are not guaranteed. If you decide to follow Jesus, that is your priority. Discipleship is a lack of material concerns.

Next, "To another he said, 'Follow me.' But he said, 'Lord, let me first go and bury my father.' But he said to him, 'Leave the dead to bury their own dead; but as for you, go and proclaim the kingdom of God' " (vv. 59-60). This is not a treatise on Christian burial or on how to take care of your relatives. This is a treatise on discipleship. The death of a father, particularly in cultures where the extended family is important, changes the entire relationship of the oldest son to the community. He now becomes the patriarch, the head of the family line. You can be sixty years old, but if your father is still alive you are a nobody. When your father dies, you become somebody. In our culture, this is still seen in royal succession. Charles is simply a prince playing games. But if his mother dies tomorrow, he suddenly becomes a mature, responsible king of England.

It may be that this disciple is saying, "Let me go back and wait till my father dies so I can have some authority and some wealth. Then I'll come and follow you." Or he may be saying, "My father has just died. I've got to go back and accept his inheritance, his responsibilities." In either case, Jesus is saying that getting such wealth or taking such responsibility is not that important if you are going to follow him, because you are going to give it all up anyway.

Even if we take this at a basic level (he simply wants to bury his father and pay his respects), following Jesus is still a more important activity and calling in life.

Lastly, "Another said, 'I will follow you, Lord; but let me first say farewell to those at my home.' Jesus said to him, 'No one who puts his hand to the plow and looks back is fit for the kingdom of God' " (vv. 61-62). The point is not that we can't shake hands and say good-by. Rather the custom in that culture was to go back and put one's affairs in order (to arrange who was going to feed the chickens, and who was going to plant the wheat in the spring, and who was going to harvest it in the fall). Then he would follow Jesus. But he would follow Jesus with the thought that maybe things were not going right back there. As soon as some rain clouds gathered, he might wonder if those kids know enough to bring the harvest in now. Or if the market changed a bit and he saw that now was the time to sell the pigs, he might start thinking to himself, "How can I get word back to them?" And Jesus does not want that kind of dual loyalty.

Once you put your hand to the plow, you keep moving.

## He Must Increase

In these six points is a definition of discipleship. While the call is ultimately to total discipleship, I also see patience on Jesus' part. "You can pick up at any level of understanding, follow me, and I will begin to teach you who I am." On several occasions throughout the ministry of Jesus, the crowd following him got large. When he intensified his teaching, many dropped off. We too need a sensitivity to call people to follow Jesus from their current understanding. But then we should bring them a fuller vision of who Jesus is and keep repeating, "Are you still willing to follow Jesus now that you've discovered more of who he really is?" Indeed, this is the question we should be asking ourselves.

Before closing, I want to go on to Luke 10. "After this the Lord appointed seventy others, and sent them on ahead of him, two by two, into every town and place where he himself was about to come" (v. 1). A very similar opening to Luke 9. But when the seventy came back, "The seventy returned with joy, saying, 'Lord, even the demons are subject to us *in your name!*' And he said to them, 'I saw Satan fall like lightning from heaven' " (vv. 17-18). In Luke 9:10, however, notice the shift of emphasis. "On their return the apostles told him what *they had done.*"

Our culture tells us to measure success by *our* accomplishments. In Luke 9 the apostles fell into the same trap. But after all the events of Luke 9, after finding out more and more of who Jesus is, the disciples have a totally different outlook. They now emphasize who Jesus is. We too will have broken the bonds of culture and moved into the realm of seeming impossibility when we thrill to what God is doing. The Word of God has made us free—free from our cultural accretions and free from Satan who is the ruler of this world. We are free from the institutions and all the propaganda. We will not only be liberated from sin, but liberated in our ability to build a style of life that meets the task of true discipleship.

The same can happen in the church. We need a community that reinforces us to live with Jesus. His values of truth and love are beyond the realm of the culturally possible. They inhabit the realm of what Jesus considers normal. Just as Jesus through the power of the Holy Spirit took the early church in Acts 1—11 step by step beyond their cultural limitations—out of Jerusalem, out of Judea, out of Samaria to the uttermost parts of the earth—so he is calling us to bring disciples out of the whole world into his church. This is true discipleship.

# Appendix
## Reaching the Campus

As an urban specialist for Inter-Varsity Christian Fellowship, I have tried to apply the model for ministry found in this book to the campus. Just as with the rest of our world, colleges and universities have been profoundly influenced by urbanization.

In the eighteen and early nineteen hundreds nearly all universities had residential campuses. Students lived together in a community separate from the rest of society. Such schools aimed to lift the student out of a provincial world view to a more cosmopolitan and sophisticated value system. Students expected to graduate with new priorities in life as well as new intellectual directions. Rarely did students return after graduation to the old community life they came from. Instead, they adopted a new culture.

In the United States this was part of the American Dream. You gave up your old culture and took on a new one. In this way education became the tool of the establishment. Anthropologically, this is a normal process. Education exists to conserve culture and pass on its values.

Today such schooling is epitomized by the Ivy League schools. Yet now, unlike the eighteen hundreds, these schools no longer dominate the university landscape. With urbanization has come the community commuter college. Instead of aiming to change the value orientation of students and move students into a new culture, commuter schools allow students to remain in their home communities and help them to be productive there. Because these students have no intention of leaving their communities, it is not surprising that they choose not to live on campus. Their primary orientation, unlike that of residential-school students, is not to the college community but to their home.

Because of urbanization, the primary community which students go back to is not necessarily their geographic community. It is more likely to be their ethnic community, their kinship community, their professional community (in the case of continuing education students) or a volunteer association such as their church. These groups set the values and agendas which students take with them to campus. While residential students are open to almost any influence imposed by their schools, commuter students come to campus to find what fits their predetermined interests and concerns.

Commuter students may change some of their values as part of their academic experience, but the pressures from the school to change are minimal. Greater influence is often exerted by peers from their home community or isolated professors crusading for particular causes. The campus as a whole limits both its value judgments on others and its concern for conformity. Unlike residential schools, commuter schools have no clear value system to pass on.

Inter-Varsity (which traces its roots to student groups active at Oxford and Cambridge nearly a hundred years ago) has traditionally worked on residential campuses. Christians from diverse church and social backgrounds came to the campus, made new friends and together developed a close evangelizing fellowship. Thus, many grew to be dedicated postcollege Christians. This was often an effective ministry because college administrators (concerned to build a new culture) were suspicious of outside influences. An indigenous group which developed from within was far less threatening to them.

With the rapid growth of commuter colleges, Inter-Varsity has had to face the challenge of reaching these as well. Unfortunately, the strategy used to reach residential schools is seldom effective in this new environment. When an urban campus is spread across a city and thus does not form a cohesive whole, how can an indigenous community be formed? When students do not even think of themselves primarily as students, how can an indigenous *student* community be formed? How can friendship evangelism take place on campus when students make most of their friends off campus?

Another problem is that in the city, a rule of survival is to never be alone. The need for community goes beyond social needs to one of self-preservation. Thus, urban students do not easily give up their group commitments. Calling a student to commitment to Christ without providing a community for protection and support may not be rational. Most successful urban ministries know the need to incarnate the gospel in a visible community. How can we take seriously existing student commitments and build a new, strong, visible community at a commuter school?

I do not know the full answers to these questions. But I believe we can begin to answer them by adopting an urban rather than a rural mindset. A rural strategy would require that the campus be the prime focus of our ministry. An urban strategy would follow the lines of communication within each cultural stripe. Our task, then, is to find and become involved with the different communities students belong to. In that setting we are more likely to win their trust and the trust of their communities.

To reach commuter schools with large Black populations, for example, we need to build especially strong relations with Black churches and pastors in the area. Since community is important to survival in the city, Black Christians may go to church four or five times a week. To reach such students, it will be helpful to go back to their community, to their church, and attend there regularly. Thus Blacks will not feel threatened that you are trying to tear them out of their church community. Likewise, Black pastors will not feel as though you are trying to steal their students. In New York City a whole group of students showed up at the Inter-Varsity meeting because their pastor told them to.

One Inter-Varsity staff member discovered that about half the Black students he was in touch with were teaching Sunday-school classes. So he gave a seminar in teaching Sunday school. The students thus saw that he had their interests and concerns in mind. He was trying to increase their contribution to the community that they cared for most.

Reversing the flow of communication can also build greater trust. Establish relationships with Black or Asian or Hispanic pastors and ask them to come on campus with you to help you reach ethnic students. They can help you overcome racial barriers, and you can help them expand the ministry of their church into a new setting. Their commitment to college work will increase not only because of their involvement but also because this can provide a new channel for more people coming into their church. Thus both church and school are strengthened.

Initially, the result of this strategy may be the development of separate, parallel communities on one campus—a Chinese Christian community, a nurses' Christian community, a Baptist Christian community and so on. But we must not leave matters there. Christ calls us to be one body. Our unity may begin along the lines of the Antioch model (Acts 13:1-3)—a leadership team made up of representatives of each major group. From there we can work to develop unity and cooperation among the group as a whole.

In addition, we will want to foster cooperation among several schools in a given area. A special interest group from one school might help begin or develop similar groups at other schools. Special areawide seminars or conferences might also be offered for Hispanic Christians or Jewish Christians, for example.

Lastly, because there is no one campus community, building Christian unity (which is so essential) will not be easy. First, it will require a higher degree of input from Inter-Varsity staff than they give to residential campuses. Second, it will take a longer period of time to establish a solid group. In New York City, for example, it has taken about five years on most campuses.

If the urban campus movement is to be an indigenous movement, support both in prayer and finances must come from the communities to which we are preparing leaders to return. But to develop this support means we must first make contributions to the prime needs of those communities.

# Notes

**Chapter 1**

[1] Arthur Glasser in *World Vision,* quoted in HIS magazine, January 1971, p. 17.

[2] Eugene Nida wrote over twenty-five years ago, "Polygamy is generally no longer treated by informed missionaries with shocked denunciations, but with an appreciative understanding of the numerous problems. More and more missions are sympathetic to permitting polygamists to become church members (but not to hold office) if such persons became polygamists before becoming acquainted with the gospel. Rather than have unwanted widows turned out to prostitution, churches have acted as sponsors of such women in arranging marriages. An awakened consciousness as to the need of educating women is changing the prevailing practice of concentrating some 90 per cent of the educational budget on training boys and men. Rather than oppose harmless but 'strange' customs approved by the people, missionaries are learning to wait and work with cultural developments." Eugene Nida, *Customs and Cultures* (New York: Harper & Brothers, 1954), pp. 264-65.

**Chapter 2**

[1] Derek Kidner, *Genesis* (Downers Grove: InterVarsity Press, 1967), p. 78.

[2] This is not controverted by the ultimate dismissal of Hagar and Ishmael in Genesis 21:8-21. In regard to 21:8, Kidner says, "Sarah spoke more truly than she knew; but the sequel shows how different was God's Spirit towards the outcasts from hers—a fact to be remembered in discussions of His sovereign will. At the close (20-21) the natural affinities of the pair are emerging, to confirm the wisdom of the parting. The story is the compliment of chapter 16, where all the parties had acted on impulse and had been recalled to live together another fourteen years or more (*cf.* 17:25). Now, with the two sons born and circumcised, God's time has ripened; *cf.* another slow maturing in 15:16." Kidner, p. 140.

[3] I do not mean to imply that marriages by choice are morally superior to marriages by arrangement. Rather, I believe God is emphasizing through the story of the patriarchs that love in marriage is a key element no matter how it may have begun.

## Chapter 3

[1]Richard R. DeRidder, *The Dispersion of the People of God* (Netherlands: J. H. Kok N. V. Kampen, 1971), p. 60.

[2]Ibid., pp. 77-83.

[3]Others identify Darius as being Cyrus himself. For a full discussion see Joyce Baldwin, *Daniel* (Downers Grove: InterVarsity Press, 1978), pp. 23-28, 119.

[4]Ronald S. Wallace, *The Lord Is King* (Downers Grove: InterVarsity Press, 1979), p. 86.

## Chapter 4

[1]DeRidder, p. 73.

[2]Ibid., pp. 71-72.

[3]Ibid., p. 10.

[4]In Ephesians 5:31-32 Paul indicates that the reverse is also true: we learn about the church through marriage. Genesis 2:24, he says, refers to Christ and the church. The community God intends is one built with the same kind of commitment and unity as marriage. The deterioration of marriage and the prevalence of divorce is tied to the deterioration of the church in the West.

## Chapter 6

[1]Joachim Jeremias suggests the population of Jerusalem swelled from approximately 25,000 to 150,000 at Passover. *Jerusalem at the Time of Jesus* (Philadelphia: Fortress, 1969), pp. 77-84.

[2]F. F. Bruce, *New Testament History* (Garden City, N.Y.: Doubleday, 1972), pp. 220-22.

[3]"Probably one synagogue is meant, although five, four, three and two have been understood by various commentators. . . . *Freedman* (Gk. *libertinoi*). Probably Jewish freedmen or descendants of freedmen from the various places mentioned." F. F. Bruce, "The Acts of the Apostles" in *The New Bible Commentary: Revised* (Grand Rapids, Mich.: Eerdmans, 1970), p. 980.

[4]Bruce, p. 218.

[5]Paul, as I indicate on pages 99-100, explains the true place of circumcision and the true meaning of Judaism in the book of Galatians.

## Chapter 7

[1]Paul elaborates on this in 1 Corinthians 8 and 10 and Romans 14:1—15:6, where he stresses Christian liberty with responsibility.

[2]While prophets certainly engaged in calling Israel to obedience (as the

priests did), I use the term *prophetic* to highlight the prophets' role in emphasizing that God was not a local deity tied to geographic Israel. Rather they clearly saw and spoke of the need to view him as a universal God who was sovereign over all nations.

## Chapter 8

[1] Kenneth Scott Latourette, *A History of Christianity,* I (New York: Harper & Row, 1975), p. xxi.

[2] Ibid., p. 330.

[3] Ibid., p. 336.

[4] Ibid., p. 414.

[5] Ibid., p. 457.

[6] Ibid., p. 404.

[7] Ralph D. Winter, *The Twenty-Five Unbelievable Years, 1945 to 1969* (Pasadena: William Carey Library, 1970), pp. 11-13.

[8] Ibid., p. 14.

[9] Kenneth Little, "Some Aspects of African Urbanization South of the Sahara," Module 5, 1971 in McCaleb Modules in Anthropology (Reading, Mass.: Addison-Wesley, 1971), p. 5-1.

[10] Advertisement, "The Think-tank Bank," *Wall Street Journal,* 3 February 1976.

[11] Richard L. Meier, *A Communications Theory of Urban Growth* (Cambridge: The M.I.T. Press, 1962), p. 13.

[12] F. Stuart Chapin, "Selected Theories of Urban Growth and Structure," in *Internal Structure of the City,* ed. Larry S. Bourne (New York: Oxford, 1971), pp. 141-53.

[13] Paul Craven and Barry Wellman, "The Network City," *Sociological Inquiry* 43 (3-4), 1973, p. 76.

[14] Meier, p. 13.

[15] Ibid., p. 14.

## Chapter 9

[1] Russell T. Hitt, "New York City: Spiritual Power Failure," *Eternity,* November 1977, pp. 37-39, 55.

[2] Amos H. Hawley, *Urban Society: An Ecological Approach* (New York: The Ronald Press, 1971), p. 9.

[3] William J. Goode, "Community within a Community: The Professions," *American Sociological Review,* April 1957, p. 194.

[4] See Kamir Olson's article on Canadian Jim Hunter, "His Pulpit: A Ski Slope," *Teen Power,* 30 November 1975, pp. 2-3, 6.

[5] Editor's note: Mafia involvement was confirmed several years later

through a report by the Pennsylvania Crime Commission entitled "Organized Crime's Infiltration of the Pizza and Cheese Industry." See James Coates, "'Pizza Wars' Bring Death to Mozarella Mobsters," *Chicago Tribune,* 24 August 1980, Section 1, p. 6.

## Chapter 10

[1] U.S. Department of Justice, Immigration and Naturalization Service, *1969 Annual Report on the Commission of Immigration and Naturalization,* Washington, D.C., U.S. Government Printing Office, 1969, p. 61.

[2] Ibid., p. 62.

[3] Nathan Glazer and Daniel Patrick Moynihan, *Beyond the Melting Pot* (Cambridge: The M.I.T. Press, 1963), p. 311.

[4] Ibid., p. 310.

[5] "The 'Irregular Economy,'" *Time* magazine, 19 February 1973, pp. 80-81.

[6] Mark Olson, "White Follies, Black Shackles," *The Other Side,* June 1979, p. 18.

[7] Ibid.

[8] Glazer and Moynihan, p. 290.

## Chapter 11

[1] John Perkins, *A Quiet Revolution* (Waco: Word, 1976), p. 33.

[2] See, for example, Psalms 25:8-10; 85:10-13; 100:5; 115:1; Proverbs 16:6 as well as those mentioned in the text.

# Suggested Reading

**Christian Social Responsibility**

Bockmuehl, Klaus. *Evangelicals and Social Ethics.* Outreach and Identity, vol. 4. Translated by David T. Priestly. Downers Grove, Ill.: InterVarsity Press, 1979.

Gladwin, John. *God's People in God's World: Biblical Motives for Social Involvement.* Downers Grove, Ill.: InterVarsity Press, 1979.

*Perkins, John. *Let Justice Roll Down: John Perkins Tells His Own Story.* Glendale, Calif.: Regal, 1976.

—————. *A Quiet Revolution: The Christian Response to Human Need. . . . A Strategy for Today.* Waco, Tex.: Word, 1976.

Sider, Ronald J., ed. *Cry Justice: The Bible Speaks on Hunger and Poverty.* Downers Grove, Ill.: InterVarsity Press, 1980.

—————. *Rich Christians in an Age of Hunger: A Biblical Study.* Downers Grove, Ill.: InterVarsity Press, 1977.

**Culture**

Kraft, Charles H. *Christianity and Culture: A Study in Dynamic Biblical Theologizing in Crosscultural Perspective.* Maryknoll, N.Y.: Orbis, 1979.

*Mayers, Marvin. *Christianity Confronts Culture: A Strategy for Crosscultural Evangelism.* Grand Rapids, Mich.: Zondervan, 1974.

*Nida, Eugene A. *Customs and Cultures: Anthropology for Christian Missions.* Pasadena: William Carey Library, 1954.

—————. *Message and Mission: The Communication of the Christian Faith.* Pasadena: William Carey Library, 1960.

*Indicates books to be read first in each category.

*Neibuhr, H. Richard, *Christ and Culture*. New York: Harper & Row, 1951.

Osseo-Asare, Francislee. *A New Land to Live In: The Odyssey of an African and American Seeking God's Guidance on Marriage*. Downers Grove, Ill.: InterVarsity Press, 1977.

Samovar, Larry A. and Porter, Richard E., eds. *Intercultural Communication: A Reader*. Belmont, Calif.: Wadsworth, 1972.

Winter, Ralph D. *The Twenty-Five Unbelievable Years: 1945-1969*. Pasadena: William Carey Library, 1970.

## General Ethnicity

*Benjamin, Barbara. *The Impossible Community*. Downers Grove, Ill.: InterVarsity Press, 1978.

Glazzer, Nathan and Moynihan, Daniel Patrick. *Beyond the Melting Pot*. 2d ed. Cambridge, Mass.: The M.I.T. Press, 1970.

Handlin, Oscar. *The Newcomers: Negroes and Puerto Ricans in a Changing Metropolis*. Cambridge, Mass.: Harvard University Press, 1959.

*Marden, Charles and Meyer, Gladys. *Minorities in American Society*. New York: D. Van Nostrand, 1978.

Novak, Michael. *The Rise of the Unmeltable Ethnics*. New York: Macmillan, 1972.

## Black Ethnicity

*The Autobiography of Malcolm X*. New York: Ballantine, 1976.

*Bennett, Lerone, Jr. *Before the Mayflower: A History of Black America*. Chicago: Johnson, 1969.

Blackwell, James. *The Black Community*. New York: Harper & Row, 1975.

Franklin, John Hope. *From Slavery to Freedom: A History of Negro Americans*. New York: Alfred A. Knopf, 1967.

King, Martin L., Jr. *Why We Can't Wait*. New York: New American Library, 1964.

*Salley, Columbus and Behm, Ron. *Your God Is Too White*. Downers Grove, Ill.: InterVarsity Press, 1970.

## Urbanization

Abrahamson, Mark. *Urban Sociology*. Englewood Cliffs, N.J.: Prentiss Hall, 1976.

*Ellison, Craig, ed. *The Urban Mission*. Grand Rapids, Mich.: Eerdmans, 1974.

Fava, Sylvia, ed. *Urbanism in World Perspective: A Reader*. New York: Harper & Row, 1968.

*Frenchak, David and Keyes, Sharrel, eds. *Metro-Ministry.* Elgin, Ill.: David C. Cook, 1979.

*Mumford, Louis, *The City in History: Its Origins, Its Transformations, and Its Prospects.* New York: Harcourt Brace Jovanovich, 1961.

Southall, Aidan, ed. *Urban Anthropology: Cross-Cultural Studies of Urbanization.* New York: Oxford University Press, 1973.

Warren, Rachelle and Warren, Donald I. *Neighborhood Organizers' Handbook.* South Bend, Ind.: University of Notre Dame Press, 1977.